LAW IN PIECES: THE GOSSIP OF HEARSAY AT SUNDAY DINNER

Anjanette G. Seymour, LL.M., LL.B. (Hons.)

This book teaches hearsay using the **Federal Rules of Evidence (FRE)**, including FRE 801–807 and related hearsay concepts discussed throughout. The characters, scenes, dialogue, and storylines in this book are fiction. Any resemblance to real persons or events is coincidental. Any trademarks, service marks, or product names referenced are the property of their respective owners. Use of such names is for identification and educational purposes only and does not imply endorsement.

This book is designed as a teaching and study supplement for students. It is not a substitute for your course materials, classroom instruction, or assigned readings. Nothing in this book is legal advice, and it does not create an attorney-client relationship. For questions about your evidence course, consult your syllabus and your professor. For legal advice about a real situation, consult a licensed attorney in the appropriate jurisdiction.

Cover design: Anjanette G. Seymour
Copyright © 2026 Anjanette G. Seymour
ISBN:9798995892328

Dedication

To all law students.

My mission is to make legal doctrines relatable—one piece at a time—so you can study with clarity, confidence, and joy. May these stories help you hear the Rules differently, and may you always consult your syllabus and your professor as you master the law.

Table of Contents

About This Book

A Sunday family gathering, in a Bahamian kitchen where everyone is cooking together — heat, noise, interruptions, side conversations and "who said what" energy. A tour of hearsay under Federal Rules of Evidence — FRE 801-807 (and the gossips in between). The goal of this book is to teach evidence hearsay through short, story-forward scenes — each chapter embodies one rule category (non-hearsay, exemptions, exceptions) or a classic problem (hearsay within hearsay).

Between chapters, being an island gal originally from The Bahamas, I have included some of our native recipes – so I am feeding not only the mind but the body as well. My characters are warm, funny, and precise just as I intended for my Law in Pieces to do — the study of law is about human interactions, I hope this book is an aid that you trust to turn to help you understand hearsay.

How to Use This Book

This is a hearsay study book disguised as a Sunday family gathering. Each scene gives you the "gossip," then pauses to translate it into the Federal Rules of Evidence—clean elements, clean purpose, and clean exam moves.

- **Rule Citations:** FRE numbers are named on purpose—so you build quick recall.
- **Elements in Plain English:** what you must show to get the statement in (or keep it out).
- **Purpose First:** every time, we ask "What is it offered to prove?" (truth vs. something else).
- **Mini-Hypos:** short variations to train issue-spotting.
- **Takeaway Cards:** memorization bullets you can reread the night before the exam.
- **Recipe Interludes:** because the kitchen is where the facts are made—and facts are where hearsay lives.
-

The Cast

(The Kitchen Is the Courtroom)

- **Cousin Kai (Narrator/Guide):** the law-school cousin who loves plain-English rules and keeps translating the kitchen talk into FRE elements.

- **Auntie Marva (The Elder / Family Historian):** remembers every version of every story—and accidentally teaches why "somebody said" is usually a problem.

- **Cousin Nia (The Skeptic):** the built-in cross-exam—always: "Who said it? When? How you know?"

- **Uncle Ro (The Fixer):** wants the statement admitted no matter what—always hunting for an exception.

- **Tia (Receipts):** screenshots, voice notes, and church programs—perfect for recorded recollection, business records vibes, and authentication arguments.

- **Little Jalen (The Blurter):** says things too fast to be strategic—present sense impressions and excited utterances happen around him.

- **Ms. Petty (The Neighbor):** pops in with "fresh news" while the oil is hot—your catalyst for spontaneity, state of mind, and layered hearsay.

- **Pastor Dean (Offstage Authority):** shows up in everyone's quotes—useful for prior statements, impeachment, and "under oath" conversations.

Roadmap (How the Book Is Organized)

Part I — Set the Table (Foundations)

1. **What Hearsay Is (and Isn't):** "Don't bring me 'somebody said.' Bring me the somebody."
2. **Why We Care:** cross-examination, perception/memory/sincerity—family kitchen version.

Part II — Not Hearsay (Because the Rules Say So)

1. **Prior Inconsistent Statement (under oath):** "Now you told the pastor one thing, but today it's another."
2. **Prior Consistent Statement:** "She been saying that from day one—before the fuss started."
3. **Prior Identification:** "That's the one. I picked him out before—same face."
4. **Opponent's Statement:** "Don't repeat what I said? Too late—you said it."
5. **Adoptive Admission:** silence at the table when accused—"You hear what she said and you ain't deny it?"
6. **Authorized/Agent/Employee Statements:** "He speaking for the whole family—he was sent to tell you."
7. **Co-conspirator Statements:** the cousins planning a surprise (or a scheme) in the pantry.

1. **Present Sense Impression:** calling out what's happening right now—"The oil too hot—look at it smoking!"
2. **Excited Utterance:** hot grease pops—somebody yelps the truth before thinking.
3. **Then-Existing State of Mind:** intentions, plans, motives—"I'm not going in that house today."
4. **Statements for Medical Diagnosis/Treatment:** a kitchen cut, urgent care story, what matters vs. what doesn't.
5. **Recorded Recollection:** the auntie's notebook—"I wrote it down because I knew I'd forget."
6. **Business Records:** receipts, store ledgers, catering invoices—regularly kept, not made for court.
7. **Public Records:** inspection reports, licenses, and official paperwork.
8. **Reputation (character / personal or family history):** "Everybody knows how Uncle is."

Part IV — When the Speaker Can't Come (Unavailability Exceptions)

1. **Former Testimony:** "We already heard him say it under oath last time."

1. **Dying Declaration:** serious moments at the edge of life—handled with care and gravity.

2. **Statement Against Interest:** "Why would she admit *that* if it wasn't true?"

3. **Personal/Family History:** births, marriages, and who's really related to who.

2. **Statement Against Interest:** "Why would she admit *that* if it wasn't true?"

3. **Personal/Family History:** births, marriages, and who's really related to who.

1. **Personal/Family History:** births, marriages, and who's really related to who.

Part V — Hearsay Within Hearsay (The Gossip Layer Cake)

1. **The Double Scoop Problem:** "My cousin said the neighbor said..."—each layer needs its own rule.
2. **Fixing the Layers:** pairing exceptions/exclusions so the whole statement can come in.
3. **When It Collapses:** one layer has no exception—so the cake falls.

Chapter 1 — What Hearsay Is (and Isn't)

Sunday starts at church for us, then soon after we are all assembled in the kitchen—pots humming, garlic bruised, and as always somebody already offended about who came empty-handed. The air got that salt-and-citrus promise, and the counters are crowded with bowls like the whole family RSVP'd at once.

"I heard he got fired," somebody says—like they sprinkling it in the pot the same way they sprinkling seasoning. Just drop it. Let it dissolve. Let everybody taste it.

The Skeptic cousin doesn't even look up from chopping onions. "You heard from *who*?"

That's the kitchen version of hearsay law—and the Federal Rules agree. Under **FRE 801(c)**, hearsay is an **out-of-court statement** offered **to prove the truth of what it asserts**. If the statement is being used for its truth, the rule's default answer is: *keep it out*—unless a rule lets it in.

But the same words can be offered for a purpose *other than* truth—and then they aren't hearsay because **FRE 801(c)** isn't triggered. In the kitchen, we do this all the time:

- **Effect on the listener:** not "was it true?" but "what did it do to them?" (why they slammed the pot, left the house, called back, or stayed quiet).
- **Notice/knowledge:** proving somebody was warned or informed (even if the warning was wrong).
- **Verbal acts / words with legal significance:** the words *are* the act (offers, acceptances, threats, permission, defamation—depending on your facts).
- **Impeachment:** using the statement to show a witness is inconsistent—not to prove the story is true.

- **Context:** giving meaning to the rest of the conversation (so the jury can understand what happened next).

Takeaway Card

- **FRE 801(a):** a "statement" can be oral, written, or nonverbal conduct intended as an assertion.

- **FRE 801(c):** hearsay = an out-of-court statement offered to prove the truth of the matter asserted.
- **Purpose is the key:** ask, "Why are we offering these words?"
- **Not-for-truth purposes** (effect on listener, notice, verbal acts, impeachment, context) often mean it's *not* hearsay.
- **If it is hearsay:** move to the next question—does FRE 801(d), 803, 804, or 807 allow it in?

Recipe 1

Dish: Bahamian-Style Fried Red Snapper

Ingredients

- 2 whole red snappers (about 1 to 1 1/2 lbs. each), cleaned and scaled
- 2 tbsp lime or lemon juice
- 1 1/2 tsp kosher salt (plus more to taste)
- 1 tsp black pepper
- 1 tsp garlic powder
- 1 tsp paprika
- 1/2 tsp dried thyme (optional)
- 1/2 cup all-purpose flour
- 1/2 cup cornmeal (or more flour if you prefer)
- Oil for frying (enough for 1/2-inch depth in a skillet)
- Optional (serve with): lime wedges, hot sauce, sliced onion, or a simple vinegar-pepper sauce

Method

1. Rinse and pat the fish dry. Score each side with 2–3 diagonal cuts.
2. Rub fish with lime/lemon juice, then season all over (and inside the cavity) with salt, pepper, garlic powder, paprika, and thyme. Let sit 10–15 minutes.
3. Mix flour and cornmeal in a shallow dish. Dredge each fish well, pressing coating into the scores.
4. Heat oil in a heavy skillet over medium-high until shimmering (a pinch of flour should sizzle immediately).
5. Fry fish 6–8 minutes per side (depending on size), until deep golden and cooked through. Transfer to a paper-towel-lined plate or rack.

6. Serve hot with peas 'n rice, fried plantain, and potato salad.

Notes: Keep the oil hot enough to fry crisp, not greasy. If your fish is large, finish in a 375°F oven for 5–8 minutes after frying to ensure it's cooked through. Drain on a rack (not just paper towels) to keep the crust crunchy.

Chapter 2 — Why We Care (Why Hearsay Gets Side-Eyed)

By the time the rice is steaming, the stories start steaming too. Auntie Marva stirring one pot, Ms. Petty stirring the room. Everybody got a version—tight, confident, and missing the one thing the Rules want most: the person who actually saw it.

Hearsay gets side-eyed because it skips the testing. In a trial, we don't just want a story—we want the chance to *test* the story. Did the speaker see it clearly (perception)? Remember it right (memory)? Tell it straight (sincerity)? Say it carefully (narration)? In the kitchen, that's Cousin Nia's whole personality: she cross-examines the gossip until it either holds up or falls apart.

So the default is caution: if you're offering an out-of-court statement for its truth, it's hearsay (**FRE 801(c)**), and you need a rule to rescue it. The exceptions aren't random—they're the law's way of saying, "Okay, we can't cross-examine this speaker right now, but something about the situation makes the statement reliable enough (or necessary enough) to let the jury hear it."

Takeaway Card

- Hearsay is treated as risky because the declarant isn't on the stand for cross-examination.
- The classic concerns: perception, memory, sincerity, and narration.
- If a statement is offered for its truth and made out of court, start with **FRE 801(c)** → then ask if **FRE 801(d), 803, 804,** or **807** saves it.
- Exceptions are about reliability/necessity substitutes— specific situations where the Rules trust the statement more than ordinary gossip.

Recipe 2

Dish: Bahamian Peas 'n Rice

Ingredients

- 2 tbsp oil (or butter)
- 1 small onion, diced
- 1 small green bell pepper, diced
- 1 stalk celery, diced
- 2 cloves garlic, minced
- 1 cup long-grain rice, rinsed
- 1 (10 oz) can pigeon peas, drained and rinsed (or black-eyed peas)
- 4 tbsps. tomato paste
- 2 cups of water
- 1 tsp fresh thyme
- 1 tsp kosher salt (to taste)
- 1/2 tsp black pepper
- Optional: 1/4 cup diced bacon or salt pork; 1 small hot pepper, whole (for flavor)

Method

1. Heat oil in a pot over medium heat. If using bacon/salt pork, cook until it starts to render, 3–5 minutes.
2. Add onion, celery, and bell pepper; cook until softened, 3–4 minutes. Add garlic and cook 30 seconds.
3. Add tomato paste and cook until most of the liquid in the pan has evaporated.
4. Add drained pigeon peas, thyme, salt, and pepper, cook for two minutes.
5. Pour in the rice and add the water. Cover. Cover the pot tightly bring to a gently boil the, reduce heat to low and

allow mixture to simmer (about 18-20 minutes) until all
the liquid has evaporated. (don't lift the lid too much).
6. Turn off heat and let sit covered 10 minutes. Fluff with a
fork and serve.

Notes: Rinsing the rice helps keep the grains separate. Don't
lift the lid too much while it cooks—steam is part of the
method. If it looks dry before tender, add 2–3 tbsp water,
cover, and keep the heat low.

Chapter 3 — The Opponent's Mouth (FRE 801(d)(2))

Ms. Petty arrives the way smoke arrives—uninvited, unmistakable, and somehow already in your clothes. She don't knock. She announces herself with news.

"Y'all heard what Rico said at the fish market?" she asks, eyes wide like she holding a plate and a secret at the same time. "He said, 'I didn't pay them because they can't do nothing to me.'"

The kitchen goes quiet in that loud way—only the oil talking now. Cousin Nia raises one eyebrow. "That's hearsay."

Cousin Kai wipes his hands because this is the kind of gossip Evidence class lives for. "Not if we offering it *against* Rico," he says. "Under **FRE 801(d)(2)**, an opposing party's statement is *not hearsay.*"

In court language, the rule is simple: if Rico is the party you're fighting, and the words came out of Rico's mouth (or his keyboard), you can use those words against him. The Rules don't treat that like ordinary hearsay because Rico can't complain about not being able to cross-examine... Rico.

Tia doesn't even speak at first. She just slides her phone across the counter, screen glowing like a tiny courtroom exhibit. A voice note is queued up. Rico's voice—clear as day, confident as sin: "Tell them I'm not paying. I'm not paying *anything.*"

Uncle Ro leans back. "And remember last week when Auntie Marva told him straight, 'You stiffed them boys, Rico,' and he just sat there chewing like the accusation was seasoning?"

Kai nods. "That's **FRE 801(d)(2)(B)**—an **adoptive admission**. If a person hears an accusation and, in context, a reasonable person would deny it, their silence—or their 'mm-hmm,' or their little shrug—can be treated like they adopted it."

Ms. Petty fans herself. "Hold on—Rico ain't even the one been talking. It was his cousin Darnell telling everybody, 'Rico said don't worry about it. Rico handling it.'"

"If Rico *authorized* Darnell to speak on his behalf," Kai says, "that's **FRE 801(d)(2)(C)**. Not 'he's family'—authorization is permission: 'You go tell them for me.'"

Uncle Ro points his spoon like a pointer. "What about when Rico's delivery guy told Mama, 'Boss said y'all can wait—he not rushing nobody'? That count?"

"That's **FRE 801(d)(2)(D)**," Kai says. "A statement made by the party's **agent or employee** on a matter within the **scope** of that relationship, while it existed. If the delivery guy is speaking about deliveries and payment—his job lane—that can come in against Rico."

Little Jalen chooses that moment to whisper, loud as a drum, "I heard Cousin Rico and Darnell in the pantry saying, 'Don't answer the phone—let it go to voicemail. If we stall long enough, they'll stop asking.'"

Kai winces, because that one comes with conditions. "That can be **FRE 801(d)(2)(E)**—a statement by a co-conspirator **during** and **in furtherance** of the conspiracy. Not just gossiping about what they already did. It has to be moving the plan forward—recruiting, coordinating, covering tracks. And you still need evidence there *was* a conspiracy and Rico was in it."

Uncle Ro smiles like he just found the missing ingredient. In this kitchen, the rule is: if it's the *opponent's* mouth (or the opponent's people speaking inside their lane), the statement isn't blocked by hearsay. The fight shifts from "hearsay!" to foundations: *who* said it, *why* they had authority, *whether* it was during and in furtherance, and whether you're truly offering it *against* the opposing party.

Takeaway Card

- **Big Rule:** Under **FRE 801(d)(2)**, certain statements are **not hearsay** when they're offered **against** an opposing party.
- **(A) Party's own statement:** the opponent said it (spoken, written, or otherwise asserted).
- **(B) Adoptive admission:** the opponent manifested adoption/belief (including silence) in circumstances where a reasonable person would deny.
- **(C) Authorized statement:** The party authorized the speaker to speak about the subject.
- **(D) Agent/employee:** statement made by agent/employee *within the scope* of the relationship and *during* the relationship.
- **(E) Co-conspirator:** statement by co-conspirator *during* and *in furtherance* of the conspiracy (requires foundation that the conspiracy existed and the party participated).

Recipe 3

Dish: Fried Plantain

Ingredients

- 3 ripe plantains (yellow with black spots for sweet), peeled and sliced on the diagonal 1/2-inch thick
- Oil for frying (about 1/2-inch depth in a skillet)
- Optional: 1–2 tsp brown sugar (for extra caramel flavor)

Method

1. Heat oil in a skillet over medium heat.

2. Fry ripe plantain slices in batches 2–3 minutes per side, until deep golden and caramelized.

3. Drain on paper towels and serve hot.

4. Drain on paper towels, sprinkle with a pinch of salt (and a little brown sugar if you like), and serve hot.

Notes: Use ripe plantains (yellow with black spots) for the best caramel flavor. Fry in batches so the oil stays hot and the edges brown evenly. Serve right away—sweet plantain is best hot.

Chapter 4 — "But You Said..." (Prior Statements: FRE 801(d)(1))

The kitchen don't just cook food—it cook alibis. By the time, the third pot is bubbling, everybody's story done seasoned itself into "facts."

Auntie Marva stands over the sink peeling potatoes like she got a contract with Sunday itself. "I *never* said Rico was at the market," she says, loud enough for the whole room. "Y'all always putting words in my mouth."

Tia looks up—slow, respectful, and deadly. "Auntie... you want to hear your own voice?" She taps her phone. Pastor Dean's Wednesday-night prayer call crackles to life, and there's Auntie Marva in surround sound: "Rico was right there by the fish stall. I saw him with my two eyes."

Cousin Nia points her knife at the speaker like it's a mic. "Hearsay."

"Not always," Kai says, sliding into his calm voice. "If the person who made the statement is a **witness**—meaning they testify—and they're **subject to cross-examination** about it, some prior statements are treated as *not hearsay* under **FRE 801(d)(1)**. The Rules basically say: 'We'll let the jury hear the earlier version, because we can still question the speaker today.'"

He nods toward Auntie Marva. "First: **FRE 801(d)(1)(A)**—a **prior inconsistent statement**. If Auntie gets on the stand today and says, 'I never said Rico was at the market,' and we can prove she said the opposite *before*, that inconsistency can come in *for its truth*—but only if the earlier statement was made **under penalty of perjury** at a **trial, hearing, or**

deposition."

Tia pauses the audio. "So the prayer call don't count for (A)?"

"Not for (A)," Kai says. "That recording can still be powerful for *impeachment*—to show Auntie's story changed. But **801(d)(1)(A)** is picky: it wants the earlier statement made in a setting where lying has teeth—oath, perjury, the whole thing."

Ms. Petty sucks her teeth. "Auntie only saying that now because she and Rico had words this morning. She mad. That's why she 'remembering' so good."

Kai lifts a finger. "Second: **FRE 801(d)(1)(B)**—a **prior consistent statement**. If the other side attacks a witness and says, 'She's making this up *now*,' or 'She got influenced,' you can sometimes answer with: 'No—she was saying the same thing *before* that motive showed up.' The idea is simple: if she said it *before* she had a reason to lie, that earlier consistency helps."

Uncle Ro snaps his fingers. "She told *me* that same thing two Sundays ago, before today's argument. Right by this same stove."

"Exactly," Kai says. "If Auntie testifies and is subject to cross, and somebody claims she's newly making it up because of a new grudge, that earlier 'I said it before the grudge' can be admitted under **801(d)(1)(B)** to set the story back on its feet."

Then Little Jalen chimes in because he always does. "Remember when the lady's purse got snatched after church and y'all asked Auntie who it was? Auntie pointed and said, 'That's him—blue hat. I know that walk.'"

Kai nods. "That's the third one: **FRE 801(d)(1)(C)**—a **prior**

identification. If a witness identifies a person after perceiving them—pointing, naming, picking from a lineup—that earlier ID can be admitted *for its truth*, as long as the witness testifies now and is subject to cross-examination. The Rules trust IDs made closer to the moment more than IDs rebuilt years later from memory and pressure."

Auntie Marva rolls her eyes like the law is something Kai made up personally. But that's the point: **801(d)(1)** is the Rules' way of saying, "We're not scared of the earlier version if the speaker is here now." If the declarant is *in the courtroom* as a witness and can be questioned, the jury can hear certain prior statements for what they're worth—because cross-examination is the antidote the Rules keep reaching for.

Takeaway Card

- **Gatekeeper requirement (all of 801(d)(1)):** the declarant must **testify** and be **subject to cross-examination** about the prior statement.
- **(A) Prior inconsistent statement:** admissible for its truth only if made **under penalty of perjury** at a **trial, hearing, or deposition**.
- **(B) Prior consistent statement:** admissible for its truth when used to **rebut** a claim of **recent fabrication** or **improper influence/motive** (and the timing matters—said before the alleged motive), and for certain rehabilitation purposes after attack.
- **(C) Prior identification:** admissible for its truth if it is an identification of a person made **after perceiving** them.
- **Quick instinct:** if the speaker is available for cross *now*, the Rules are more willing to let the jury hear the "older version" of the story.

Recipe 4

Dish: Bahamian-Style Potato Salad

Ingredients

- 2 1/2 lbs. russet or Yukon Gold potatoes, peeled and cut into 1-inch chunks
- 1 tbsp kosher salt (for boiling water), plus more to taste
- 4 large eggs
- 1 cup mayonnaise
- 2 tbsp yellow mustard
- 2 tbsp sweet relish
- 1/2 cup diced onion
- 1/2 cup diced celery (optional)
- 1/2 cup diced bell pepper (green or red)
- 1/2 tsp black pepper
- 1/2 tsp paprika (plus more for top)
- Optional: 1 tbsp white vinegar or pickle juice (for brightness)

Method

1. Place potatoes in a pot, cover with cold water, add 1 tbsp salt, and bring to a boil. Simmer until fork-tender, 10–12 minutes. Drain and let cool.
2. Hard-boil eggs: cover eggs with water, bring to a boil, turn off heat, cover 10–12 minutes. Cool, peel, and chop.
3. In a large bowl, whisk mayo, mustard, relish, black pepper, and paprika (and vinegar/pickle juice if using).
4. Fold in potatoes, eggs, onion, bell pepper (and celery if using). Taste and adjust salt/pepper.

5. Chill at least 1 hour. Sprinkle a little paprika on top
    before serving.

Notes: Don't overcook the potatoes—slightly firm pieces hold
their shape. Chill at least 1 hour so the flavors set before
serving. A splash of vinegar or pickle juice brightens the bowl,
especially next to fried fish.

Recipe 5

Dish: Guava Duff (with Hard Sauce)

Ingredients

- 12 medium guavas, peeled
- 4 cups all-purpose flour (plus more for rolling)
- 3 tsps. baking powder
- 1 tsp salt
- ½ cup sugar
- 1 tsp cinnamon
- 1 tsp allspice, ground
- 3/4 cup shortening
- 3/4 cup milk (plus a splash more if needed)
- 1 egg, beaten

Method

1. Peel guavas, cut in half and remove seeds.
2. Dice the fruit and strain to remove juice. Save juice to flavor sauce if desired. Put fruit in saucepan with water to cover; add sugar, cinnamon, and allspice. Simmer fruits until soft.
3. Combine flour, baking powder, and salt. Cut in shortening. Stir in milk and egg to form a soft dough.
4. Kneed until smooth. Roll out like a jelly roll on floured board.
5. Place ½ of the guava pieces on the center 1/3 of the dough and fold over 1/3. Place remaining guava on folded dough and fold over the other 1/3 and seal edges carefully.
6. Wrap dough in a cotton or linen bag, or foil, tie the top securely and put into a large pot of boiling water, or a double boiler. Boil for 1 hour or more if necessary to set duff.
7. Serve with hard sauce.
8. Mix flour, baking powder, salt, and sugar. Rub in butter, then stir in milk to make a soft dough.

9. Roll dough into a rectangle about 1/4 inch thick. Place guava paste (and raisins) down the center, roll up, and pinch seams closed.
10. Wrap tightly in a clean cloth and tie the ends. Boil gently 45–60 minutes, turning once or twice.
11. Unwrap, slice, and serve.
12. Butter sauce: melt butter on low heat, stir in sugar, add evaporated milk and vanilla, and stir until smooth and warm.

Hard Sauce:

Ingredients

- 1 cup confectioners sugar
- ¼ cup butter
- 1 tsp. boiling water
- Dash of salt
- 2 tbsps. Brandy or rum.

Method

1. Cream butter until soft not melted.
2. Beat in confectioners sugar gradually.
3. Add boiling water, salt, and brandy or rum.
4. Beat until smooth and fluffy.
5. Makes 1 cup

Notes: Keep the boil gentle so the duff doesn't burst. Serve warm with hard sauce—this is the dessert that quiets a room.

Chapter 5 — The Oil Don't Lie (Present Sense Impression: FRE 803(1))

When the red snapper hits the skillet, the kitchen becomes a language all by itself—sizzle, pop, spit. Everybody suddenly got expert ears. Everybody suddenly got an opinion.

"Oil too hot," Auntie Marva says without looking up. "Hear that? It talking angry."

Little Jalen stands on a chair to see. "It's smoking! The flour turning brown already!"

Cousin Nia, because she can't help herself, says, "If Jalen run to court later and says, 'Auntie told me the oil was too hot,' that's hearsay."

Kai shrugs. "It can be—unless it fits **FRE 803(1)**. A **present sense impression** is a statement describing or explaining an event or condition, made while the declarant is perceiving it or immediately after. The law trusts the timing. There's no time to sit down, edit the story, or add sauce."

He points at the pan. "Right now: 'The snapper is sticking.' 'The plantains are burning.' That's description. But if Auntie disappears, takes a phone call, and fifteen minutes later announces, 'The oil was too hot because Nia always rushing,' now we've got distance—time for interpretation, blame, and family politics."

Takeaway Card

- **FRE 803(1):** statement **describing or explaining** an event/condition, made **while perceiving it** or **immediately after**.
- **Timing is everything:** the longer the gap, the weaker the fit.
- **Stick to description:** "It's smoking" fits better than "She did it on purpose."
- **No unavailability required:** FRE 803 exceptions apply regardless of whether the declarant can testify.

Recipe 6

Dish: Quick Vinegar-Pepper Sauce (for Fried Snapper)

Ingredients

- 1/2 cup white vinegar
- 1/4 cup water
- 1 small hot pepper (goat pepper or habanero), sliced (use less for mild)
- 2 tbsp sliced onion
- 1/2 tsp kosher salt
- 1/2 tsp sugar (optional)
- Optional: 1 clove garlic, smashed; 4 whole peppercorns

Method

1. Combine vinegar, water, pepper, onion, salt (and sugar/garlic/peppercorns if using) in a jar.
2. Shake and let sit at least 15 minutes (better after 1 hour).
3. Spoon a little over fried snapper right before serving.

Notes: Start with a little—vinegar cuts through fried food fast. Let it sit at least 15 minutes so the flavors mellow. Keeps in the fridge about 1 week.

Chapter 6 — Grease Pop Truth (Excited Utterance: FRE 803(2))

The snapper fights back sometimes. One wrong tilt of the pan, and the oil jumps like it got feelings. That's when truth comes out the same way yelps come out—fast, raw, and not planned.

Oil pops. Little Jalen jerks his hand back. "Auntie! Nia pushed me into the stove!" he blurts, eyes wide, clutching his fingers like they're evidence.

"I did *not*," Nia says, already building her defense like she's filing motions.

Kai points at Jalen's shaking hand. "This is where **FRE 803(2)** lives. An **excited utterance** is a statement relating to a startling event or condition, made while the declarant is still under the stress of excitement caused by it. The rule trusts the adrenaline. The moment is doing the talking, not a rehearsal."

Later, after Jalen's calm and eating plantain, if he tells the story again with flourishes—who looked guilty, who had an attitude, what Mama "always does"—that's when the exception starts slipping. The calmer the teller gets, the more the statement starts sounding like ordinary kitchen testimony instead of a reflex.

Takeaway Card

- **FRE 803(2):** statement **relating to** a startling event/condition, made while still under the **stress of excitement** caused by it.
- **Timing is flexible:** the key is whether the declarant is still "lit up" by the event.
- **Watch the shift:** once the speaker calms down, starts reasoning, or starts crafting a narrative, the exception weakens.

Recipe 7

Dish: Lime-Honey Drizzle (for Fried Sweet Plantains)

Ingredients

- 3 tbsp honey
- 1 tbsp fresh lime juice
- 1/2 tsp lime zest (optional)
- Pinch of salt
- Optional: pinch of cayenne or crushed red pepper

Method

1. Whisk honey, lime juice, zest, and salt (and cayenne if using) until smooth.
2. Drizzle lightly over hot fried sweet plantains right before serving.

Notes: Drizzle lightly—sweet plantains already caramelize. The lime keeps it bright, and the pinch of salt makes the sweetness pop. Best right on the hot plantains.

Chapter 7 — "I'm Not Sitting By Him" (State of Mind: FRE 803(3))

Potato salad is where grudges go to hide. Everybody stirring, tasting, and pretending the bowl is the only thing they need to control.

Auntie Marva wipes her hands and says, flat and final: "I'm not sitting by Rico today. And I'm not taking a plate to him neither."

Kai nods like he's been waiting on that sentence. "That's **FRE 803(3)**. A statement of the declarant's **then-existing** state of mind—motive, intent, plan—or emotional/physical condition can come in. 'I'm not sitting by him.' 'I'm leaving.' 'I'm going to the fish market.' The rule trusts what people say about what they feel or plan *right now*."

But Kai holds up a warning hand. "What the rule doesn't let you do is sneak in a whole history lesson. If Auntie says, 'I'm not sitting by him *because he threatened me last week*,' the 'I'm not sitting by him' part is state of mind. The 'he threatened me' part is a memory offered to prove a past fact—and that's exactly the kind of thing hearsay loves to smuggle."

Takeaway Card

- **FRE 803(3):** statements of **then-existing** state of mind (motive, intent, plan) or emotional/physical condition are admissible.
- **Use it to show "what they meant to do":** intent/plan can help prove later actions.
- **Limit:** not statements of **memory or belief** to prove the fact remembered/believed (except certain will-related issues).

Recipe 8

Dish: Pepper-Sauce Potato Salad (Sunday Remix)

Ingredients

- 4 cups prepared potato salad (use Recipe 4)
- 1–2 tsp Bahamian-style pepper sauce (to taste)
- 1 tbsp pickle juice or white vinegar (optional, for brightness)
- Paprika, for top

Method

1. Stir pepper sauce into chilled potato salad, starting with 1 tsp. Taste and add more if you want heat.
2. If needed, add pickle juice/vinegar to brighten.
3. Chill 30 minutes, then dust the top with paprika.

Notes: Add pepper sauce slowly and taste as you go—heat grows as it sits. Chill at least 30 minutes after mixing so the flavor spreads through the bowl. This one is made for fried snapper plates.

Chapter 8 — "Tell the Nurse What Happened" (Medical Diagnosis/Treatment: FRE 803(4))

Some Sundays, the evidence comes with a bandage. Between the snapper oil and the plantain oil, somebody always gets a little too brave.

Auntie Marva sits Jalen at the table and runs cool water over his hand. "When the nurse ask, you tell her exactly where it hurts and what touched you," she says. "Don't be adding no drama."

Kai nods. "That's **FRE 803(4)**. Statements made for—and reasonably pertinent to—medical diagnosis or treatment can come in: symptoms, pain, what happened, even the general cause. The rule assumes people are motivated to tell the truth when they're trying to get help."

He looks at Jalen. "So 'Hot oil splashed my hand when the pan tipped' is the kind of cause a nurse needs. But 'Nia did it on purpose' is blame—usually not pertinent to treatment. The question is always: would a medical professional reasonably need this information to diagnose or treat?"

Takeaway Card

- **FRE 803(4):** statements made for—and reasonably pertinent to—medical diagnosis or treatment.
- **What fits:** symptoms, pain, sensations, medical history, and general cause (what touched you, where, when).
- **Watch blame/identity:** who caused it is usually not pertinent (unless the identity itself is medically relevant in your fact pattern).

Recipe 9

Dish: Coconut Peas 'n Rice (Sunday Variation)

Ingredients

- 1 cup long-grain rice, rinsed
- 1 (10 oz) can pigeon peas, drained and rinsed
- 3/4 cup canned coconut milk
- 3/4 cup chicken broth or water
- 1/2 cup tomato sauce
- 1/2 tsp dried thyme
- 1 tsp kosher salt (to taste)
- 1/2 tsp black pepper
- Optional: 1 small whole hot pepper

Method

1. Combine rice, peas, coconut milk, broth/water, tomato sauce, thyme, salt, pepper (and whole hot pepper if using) in a pot.
2. Bring to a gentle boil, reduce to low, cover, and simmer 18–20 minutes.
3. Turn off heat and rest covered 10 minutes. Fluff and serve.

Notes: Coconut milk gives the rice a richer Sunday feel without changing the technique. Keep the heat low so it doesn't scorch. If it thickens too early, add 1–2 tbsp water and cover.

Chapter 9 — "It's in My Book" (Recorded Recollection: FRE 803(5))

Auntie Marva keeps the Sunday spread the way some people keep secrets—locked up, measured, and written down. Not in a phone. Not in the cloud. In a battered notebook with flour on the corners and oil fingerprints on the truth.

Today it's the snapper that starts the argument. The fish market had the good ones, and everybody watching the skillet like it's a championship. Nia says, "Auntie, you always over-salt the fish." Uncle Ro says, "No she don't—she just don't measure." Tia says, "She do measure. She just don't tell *y'all*."

Auntie Marva opens her mouth to end it, then pauses—because even legends forget numbers sometimes. "Hold on," she says, patting her apron like she's looking for a pen. "I wrote it down."

She flips to a page titled in heavy handwriting: "*SUNDAY: SNAPPER + PEAS 'N RICE + PLANTAIN + POTATO SALAD.*" Right under it: little lines, little ratios, little warnings—"don't crowd the pan," "let rice rest," "taste potato salad *cold.*"

Kai nods like he just got handed a rulebook and a plate. "This is **FRE 803(5)—Recorded Recollection**. Sometimes a witness is honest and present, but their memory is not. If a witness **once knew** the information but now **can't recall well enough to testify fully and accurately**, a record can step in—*if* it was **made or adopted** when the matter was fresh and it **accurately reflects** the witness's knowledge."

Auntie clears her throat and reads, slow and satisfied: "Two fish. Lime first. Salt one-and-a-half teaspoons, pepper one teaspoon, garlic one teaspoon, paprika one teaspoon... dredge, fry, don't talk to me while I'm flipping."

"In court," Kai says, "the record usually comes in by being **read into evidence**. The jury gets the words, not necessarily the paper. The paper itself only becomes an exhibit if the other side wants it that way."

Nia squints. "So this is different than just showing her the notebook to jog her memory?"

"Exactly," Kai says. "If she reads it and suddenly remembers, then she testifies from memory—that's refreshing recollection. But if she still can't remember the exact amounts without the page, the page can speak under **803(5)**, as long as it was made when things were fresh and it's accurate."

Takeaway Card

- **FRE 803(5):** recorded recollection.
- **Requirements:** (1) witness once knew; (2) now can't recall well enough to testify fully/accurately; (3) record was made/adopted when fresh; (4) record accurately reflects the witness's knowledge.
- **How it comes in:** the record is **read into evidence**; it's an exhibit only if the adverse party offers it.
- **Compare:** refreshed recollection = witness testifies from revived memory; recorded recollection = record substitutes for missing memory.

Recipe 10

Dish: Auntie Marva's Snapper Seasoning Mix (Notebook Blend)

Ingredients

- 2 tbsp kosher salt
- 1 tbsp black pepper
- 1 tbsp garlic powder
- 1 tbsp paprika
- 1 tsp dried thyme
- Optional: 1 tsp onion powder; 1/2 tsp cayenne

Method

1. Mix everything in a small jar.
2. For 2 whole snappers, start with 2–3 tsp seasoning mix total (plus lime), then adjust to taste.
3. Rub onto fish before dredging and frying.

Notes: Keep it in a jar and you're always close to Sunday snapper. Start light—salt is already in the blend—and adjust on the fish. Lime goes on first for brightness.

Chapter 10 — Receipts Don't Gossip (Business Records: FRE 803(6))

If the kitchen is where the gossip lives, the fish market is where it starts. The snapper just doesn't appear. Somebody paid. Somebody signed. Somebody got change back.

Tia lays a long, curled receipt on the counter like it's a ribbon of facts. "Two red snappers. Ice. Lime. Oil. Plantains. And look—potatoes, eggs, mayo, mustard. Time-stamped. Paid."

Nia tilts her head. "That's an out-of-court statement on paper. Hearsay."

Kai smiles. "Normally, yes. But **FRE 803(6)** is the business world's way of saying: some paper isn't gossip—it's routine. A **record of a regularly conducted activity** can come in if it was made **at or near the time** by someone with knowledge, kept in the **course** of a regularly conducted business activity, and making that kind of record is a **regular practice**. Then you need a custodian or other qualified witness to lay the foundation—and the opponent can still argue it's untrustworthy."

Uncle Ro—who always finds himself acting like a witness even when he came for a plate—taps the receipt. "That market print those every sale. They don't type it special because *we* arguing in this kitchen."

Tia flips to another page—an invoice from Auntie Marva's little catering run: "*Sunday Plates: Fried Snapper / Peas 'n Rice / Plantain / Potato Salad — 25 orders.*" It lists a pickup time, a phone number, and a total that makes everybody suddenly respectful. That's the heart of 803(6): records made to run a business—track money, track inventory, track deliveries—carry a kind of built-in discipline.

Ms. Petty tries to lean in with a handwritten note on looseleaf—no date, no letterhead, just attitude: "Rico owe everybody." Kai side-eyes it. "A record isn't a business record just because it's written down. If it's made for a fight—made when the arguing starts—it's not routine, and courts worry about trustworthiness."

Takeaway Card

- **FRE 803(6):** records of a regularly conducted activity (business records).
- **Foundation (core idea):** routine records are trusted more than one-off storytelling.
- **Elements to hit:** made at/near the time; by (or from information transmitted by) someone with knowledge; kept in the course of regularly conducted activity; making it was a regular practice; shown by custodian/qualified witness (or certification).
- **Escape hatch:** excluded if circumstances show a lack of trustworthiness.

Recipe 11

Dish: Fish Market Order List (Signature Sunday Spread for 8)

Ingredients

- 4 whole red snappers (about 1–1 1/2 lbs. each) or 8 snapper fillets
- 6–8 limes
- Oil for frying (about 6–8 cups, depending on pan size and depth)
- Flour (2 cups) + cornmeal (2 cups)
- Plantains: 8 ripe (or mix ripe + green)
- Rice: 4 cups long-grain
- Pigeon peas: 2 cans (15 oz each)
- Tomato sauce: 1 cup
- Potatoes: 5 lb.
- Eggs: 12
- Mayo: 2 cups; mustard: 1/4 cup; relish: 1/4 cup
- Onions: 2; bell peppers: 2; garlic: 1 head
- Hot peppers (goat pepper/habanero), optional

Method

1. Boil potatoes and eggs first; chill potato salad while you cook everything else.
2. Start peas 'n rice next (it can rest covered and stay perfect).
3. Season and dredge snapper; set up your "fry station" (rack/paper towels, tongs, thermometer if you use one).
4. Fry plantains in batches; keep warm.
5. Fry snapper last so it hits the table crisp.

Notes: This order list keeps Sunday smooth: prep cold items first, cook rice early, fry fish last. Save the receipts—future you will thank you. If snapper prices jump, adjust quantity, not tradition.

Chapter 11 — The Missing Receipt (Absence of a Record: FRE 803(7))

In this family, receipts are the grown-up version of "don't play with me." If you say you bought four red snappers, Tia wants the paper. If you say you paid for twenty-five Sunday plates, Uncle Ro wants the invoice. Because gossip can lie—paper usually don't.

That's why the room gets loud when Rico says, casual as a shrug, "I already paid the fish market last week. They owe *me*."

Tia starts scrolling—photos, emails, bank alerts, the whole archive. Then she goes quiet. "Funny," she says. "Because I can find *every* time we bought snapper. I can find oil, plantains, potatoes, eggs, and mayo. But I can't find a single receipt where Rico paid anything 'last week.'"

Kai nods. "That absence can matter. **FRE 803(7)** lets you prove that something *didn't happen*—or that a certain record *doesn't exist*—by showing the matter is missing from records that are regularly kept. If a business regularly makes and keeps records of sales and payments, and a particular payment isn't there, the Rules let that 'missing entry' speak."

Uncle Ro adds, "Same with Auntie's catering book. If she logs every Sunday plate order—snapper, peas 'n rice, plantain, potato salad—and there's no entry for 'Rico paid,' that silence can be evidence too."

But Kai holds up the same caution he always does: the system has to be real. If the business is sloppy, if records go missing all the time, if people don't regularly record that kind of transaction, then the absence is less meaningful. The Rules still care about trustworthiness—even when you're proving a negative.

Uncle Ro takes a break from arguing to rescue his Switcha—
cold from the fridge, sweating down the sides of that old tin
can cup he swears tastes better than any glass. He drinks,
thinks, then says, "See? Even the missing paper telling a story.
Sometimes silence is the loudest witness."

Takeaway Card

- **FRE 803(7):** absence of an entry in records kept under
  FRE 803(6).
- **Use:** to prove the **nonoccurrence** or **nonexistence**
  of a matter.
- **Foundation:** show the business regularly kept records
  of that kind, and the matter would normally be
  recorded.
- **Still defeatable:** absence is weaker if the system is
  sloppy or circumstances suggest untrustworthiness.

Recipe 12

Dish: Switcha (Bahamian Lemonade)

Ingredients

- 1 cup fresh-squeezed lemon juice (about 6–8 lemons)
- 3/4 cup granulated sugar (adjust to taste)
- 6 cups cold water
- Ice for serving
- Optional: lemon slices

Method

1. In a pitcher, stir lemon juice and sugar until the sugar dissolves.
2. Add cold water, stir, and taste. Add more sugar for sweeter, more water for lighter.
3. Chill in the fridge at least 1 hour. Serve over ice.

Notes: Chill it at least an hour for the cleanest lemon flavor. Taste before serving—lemons vary—then adjust sugar or water. Uncle Ro swears it tastes colder in his tin can.

Chapter 12 — The Inspector's Paperwork (Public Records: FRE 803(8))

The fish market isn't just vibes and ice. It's rules. Permits. Inspections. Somebody in an office somewhere deciding whether the snapper gets sold or gets tossed.

Ms. Petty waves her hand over the fried snapper like she blessing it and shading it at the same time. "I heard that market get wrote up all the time. That's why the fish taste 'funny.'"

Tia doesn't argue. She prints. "Here," she says, dropping a stapled report on the table beside the potato salad. "Inspection score. Dates. Notes. Signed."

Kai nods. "That's **FRE 803(8)—Public Records**. A record or statement of a public office can come in if it sets out the office's activities, matters observed under a legal duty to report, or factual findings from an authorized investigation—so long as the circumstances don't show it's untrustworthy."

He adds, careful: "And the Rules put extra limits on certain law-enforcement-type observations in criminal cases. But for everyday public-office paperwork—licenses, inspection reports, permits—803(8) is often the clean path."

Takeaway Card

- **FRE 803(8):** public records.
- **Covers:** records of a public office setting out (A) its activities; (B) matters observed under a legal duty to report; (C) factual findings from a legally authorized investigation.

- **Trustworthiness still matters:** the opponent can show circumstances indicate a lack of trustworthiness.
- **Remember limits:** some law-enforcement observations have special restrictions in criminal cases.

Recipe 13

Dish: Lattice Coconut Tart

Ingredients

- **Crust:** 2 1/2 cups all-purpose flour; 1 tbsp sugar; 1/2 tsp salt; 1 cup (2 sticks) cold butter, cubed; 6–8 tbsp ice water
- **Filling:** 3 cups sweetened shredded coconut; 1 cup evaporated milk; 3/4 cup sugar; 2 tbsp butter; 2 large eggs; 1 tsp vanilla; 1/4 tsp nutmeg (optional); pinch of salt
- **Finish:** 1 egg (beaten) for egg wash; 1 tbsp sugar to sprinkle (optional)

Method

1. Crust: In a bowl, mix flour, sugar, and salt. Cut in cold butter until crumbly with pea-size bits. Add ice water 1 tbsp at a time until the dough just comes together. Divide dough into two pieces (one slightly larger). Wrap and chill 30 minutes.
2. Filling: In a saucepan over medium-low heat, warm evaporated milk, sugar, and butter until melted and combined. Remove from heat. Stir in coconut, vanilla, nutmeg (if using), and a pinch of salt. Let cool 5–10 minutes, then stir in eggs.
3. Preheat oven to 375°F. Roll the larger dough piece and fit into a 9-inch tart pan (or pie dish). Trim edges.
4. Pour coconut filling into the crust and smooth the top.
5. Lattice: Roll the remaining dough and cut into 1/2-inch strips. Lay strips across the tart and weave into a lattice. Brush lattice with egg wash and sprinkle with a little sugar if desired.
6. Bake 35–45 minutes, until the lattice is golden and the filling is set. If the top browns too fast, tent loosely with foil.
7. Cool at least 30 minutes before slicing so the filling firms up.

Notes: Chill the dough so the lattice stays flaky. Let the filling cool slightly before adding eggs so they don't scramble. Slice after it rests so the coconut sets clean.

Chapter 13 — Church Program Proof (Vital Statistics & No Record Found: FRE 803(9)–(10))

By the time the lattice coconut tart cools, the kitchen quiets down just enough for somebody to pull out paper.

Not a receipt. Not an invoice. A church program—folded in half, smudged with potato-salad fingerprints. Tia sets it on the table like a deposition exhibit. "Read it," she says. "Right there under 'Announcements.'"

Auntie Marva reads aloud while handing out leftover snapper like communion: *"We joyfully announce the marriage of…"* She stops mid-sentence. "Hold on. *Marriage?*"

Ms. Petty leans in so fast her earrings almost hit the tart. "Chile, church paper ain't proof. People will announce anything. Next thing you know, somebody 'married' and still got a boyfriend."

Nia squints at the program. "Out-of-court statement offered to prove the truth—sounds like hearsay to me."

Kai nods. "The church program is gossip-adjacent. The *real* hearsay answer is the government paper. **FRE 803(9)** covers **public records of vital statistics**—births, deaths, and **marriages**—if the record is reported to a public office under a legal duty."

He points with a fork because that's the only pointer available. "And **FRE 803(10)** is the flip side—when you need to prove a matter *didn't* happen, you can offer evidence that a diligent search found **no public record**. In other words: 'We checked the marriage records, and there is no marriage record for them.'"

Tia, of course, already did the homework. She taps her folder—yes, a literal folder in a family kitchen. "Either they're married, and the certificate is on file," she says, "or they're not, and the clerk says there's no record." Uncle Ro takes a sip of Switcha from his tin can and mutters, "If it ain't on paper, it ain't on *paper*."

Takeaway Card

- **FRE 803(9):** public records of **vital statistics** (birth, death, marriage) reported to a public office under a legal duty.
- **FRE 803(10):** absence of a public record—evidence that a diligent search found **no record** where one would normally exist.
- **Kitchen translation:** the church program starts the gossip, but the clerk's record (or "no record found") finishes the proof.

Recipe 14

Dish: Switcha (Crowd Pitcher for Church Sunday)

Ingredients

- 2 cups fresh-squeezed lemon juice (about 12–16 lemons)
- 1 1/2 cups granulated sugar (adjust to taste)
- 12 cups cold water
- Ice for serving
- Optional: lemon slices

Method

1. In a large pitcher, stir lemon juice and sugar until dissolved.
2. Add cold water, stir, and taste. Adjust sugar or water until it tastes like Sunday.
3. Chill in the fridge at least 1–2 hours. Serve over ice.

Notes: Chill at least 1–2 hours so it tastes clean, not sharp. Serve ice on the side so nobody complains it's watered down. Uncle Ro still uses his tin can for the coldest sip.

Chapter 14 — Certified and Sealed (Certified Records: FRE 803(11)–(12))

The whole family loves "proof"… until proof has to come from somebody who ain't here. Because the clerk who keeps the marriage records is not coming to Sunday dinner, and the fish market cashier is not leaving work to testify about a receipt you already paid for.

Kai taps the edge of Tia's folder. "This is where the Rules get practical. **FRE 803(11)** and **803(12)** let certain **certified records** come in—domestic and foreign—without dragging the custodian into court, so long as the certification shows the record meets the business-record foundation and the other side gets proper notice."

Tia flips to the page with the stamp—raised seal, official signature. Uncle Ro nods like he's approving a fry temperature. "That's what I'm talking about. Not 'my friend said.' Not 'I saw it online.' *Stamped.*"

Same idea for the Sunday spread business: if the catering invoices and delivery logs are true business records, a proper certification can stand in for live testimony. The Rules aren't lowering the bar—they're changing the messenger. You still need the same reliability story; you just don't need the cashier to tell it when the paperwork already does.

Takeaway Card

- **FRE 803(11)–(12):** certain **certified records** (domestic and foreign) can be admitted without live custodian testimony.
- **Core idea:** the certification substitutes for the custodian, but the record must still satisfy the reliability/foundation requirements.

- **Practice point:** notice matters—opposing parties must have a fair chance to inspect and challenge.

Chapter 15 — "It's in the Family Bible" (Family Records: FRE 803(13))

After the church program and the clerk talk, the kitchen does what it always does: it turns into an archive. Plates of leftover snapper sit on the counter like exhibits waiting to be marked. The peas 'n rice is packed into a container. The plantains are covered with foil. And Auntie Marva—quiet now—goes to the drawer everybody knows about.

It's not a fancy drawer. It's the "don't-touch-that" drawer. The family Bible is in there, thick, and soft at the corners, with paper tucked into it the way other people tuck money. Old funeral programs. Baptism cards. A yellowed wedding announcement. A page where somebody, long ago, wrote names in careful handwriting: *Married: ____ / ____.*

Auntie Marva sets the Bible down like she's setting down a judge. "Y'all want to argue marriage?" she says. "Look. We been writing our people down before y'all learned how to screenshot."

Nia leans in because rules don't stop being rules just because the paper is holy. "Still an out-of-court statement, Auntie. Still offered for its truth."

Kai nods. "And that's exactly why **FRE 803(13)** exists. It lets in a **statement of fact about personal or family history** when it's contained in a **family record**—like a family Bible, a genealogy, a chart, a ring inscription, even something stitched into a quilt—things families keep because they're trying to remember, not because they're trying to win a lawsuit."

The point isn't that families never get anything wrong. The point is that families keep these records to *remember*. They get updated at births, at funerals, at weddings—when nobody is thinking about court. That regular, life-driven habit is what gives the record its weight.

So if the question is, "Were they married?" the family Bible entry can be one path under **803(13)**. The church program might start the talk, the clerk's certificate might end it, but the family record sits in the middle as the thing your people have been keeping—quietly— long before anybody started arguing about proof.

Takeaway Card

- **FRE 803(13):** statements of fact about **personal or family history** contained in a **family record**.
- **Family record examples:** family Bible, genealogy, chart, ring inscription, engraving, tombstone inscription, or similar family-maintained record.
- **Why it works:** these records are usually kept to remember life events—not to win a case.
- **Still watch trust:** if it looks like it was created for litigation or "after the fight started," the judge/jury will be skeptical.

Recipe 15

Dish: Auntie Marva's Recipe Card Box (The Family Record
Behind the Sunday Spread)

Ingredients

- 1 battered recipe-card box (or envelope) that everybody
  knows not to "borrow"
- Cards labeled: *Fried Snapper, Peas 'n Rice, Fried
  Plantain, Potato Salad*
- One "special occasions" divider: *Guava Duff, Lattice
  Coconut Tart*, and whatever Auntie refuses to share
- A pencil (not pen)—because Auntie edits with the
  seasons

Method

1. Write it down the day it works—while the oil is still hot
   and the rice is still steaming.
2. Date the tweak ("more lime," "less salt," "don't crowd
   the pan") so Sunday doesn't become guesswork.
3. Keep the cards where they live—near the kitchen, not
   lost in a phone upgrade.
4. Let the next cook follow the card once before they
   freestyle—because that's how tradition survives.

Notes: Write the tweak down while you can still taste it. Date
your changes so "always" has receipts. This box is tradition in
ink.

Chapter 16 — "Whose House Is That?" (Property Records: FRE 803(14))

Sunday plates make people brave. A full belly will have you asking questions you should've left alone—especially when the church program already started a marriage argument.

Ms. Petty holds a piece of fried snapper like a microphone. "Okay, since everybody announcing weddings now—who house she living in?"

Auntie Marva stops mid-stir on the peas 'n rice. Nia's eyes narrow. Uncle Ro laughs once—short. "Don't do that," he says. "Don't start counting people blessings with potato salad on your fork."

But Tia is already doing what she does—finding paper. She slides her phone across the counter, not a screenshot of gossip this time, but a PDF with a stamp line and a recording number. "This is the deed that's filed," she says. "Recorded. Public. Dated."

Kai nods. "This is where **FRE 803(14)** comes in—**Records of documents that affect an interest in property**. When a document like a deed, mortgage, or lien is recorded in a public office, the *record* of that document can be admitted to prove the content of the original."

In kitchen terms: this isn't "Ms. Petty heard." This is the county saying, "Here is what was filed." The recording system exists to track ownership and notice to the world, so the Rules treat those recorded property records like a dependable source for what the document says.

- **FRE 803(14):** the **record** of a document that affects an interest in property is admissible to prove the **content** of the original recorded document.
- **Think:** deeds, mortgages, liens, recorded easements—documents filed in a public office.
- **Why it works:** recording systems exist to track ownership/notice, so the records are treated as reliable for what the document says.

Chapter 17 — The Deed Talks Too (Statements in Property Documents: FRE 803(15))

Tia scrolls, zooms, and reads the line everybody cares about—the part where the names live. Because names on paper settle arguments faster than voices in a kitchen.

Kai points at the screen. "Now we're in **FRE 803(15)**. It's not just the *record* of the deed—sometimes it's the *statements inside* a document that affects an interest in property. If the statement is relevant to the property interest, and later dealings with the property have been consistent with the statement, the Rules will let the document speak."

That's why deeds talk about more than who bought the house. They talk about boundaries, easements, who has rights to what, sometimes even who inherits what happens next. And if everybody's been treating the property like the deed says—paying taxes, living there, renting it out—then the paper looks less like a story and more like a settled fact.

Takeaway Card

- **FRE 803(15):** statements in a document that affects an interest in property are admissible if the statement is relevant to the interest and later dealings with the property are consistent with it.
- **Think:** deeds, mortgages, leases, easements—documents where people memorialize property rights.
- **Reliability hook:** property paper tends to get relied on over time; consistency in later conduct supports trust.

Recipe 16

Dish: Uncle Ro's Tin-Can Switcha Chill (Lunch Tradition)

Ingredients

- 2 cups prepared Switcha (see Recipe Interlude 12 or 14)
- 1 clean tin can cup (Uncle Ro-approved)
- Fridge time (at least 45 minutes)
- Optional: ice, for serving

Method

1. Pour Switcha into the tin can cup.
2. Set it in the fridge while the Sunday plates get packed up (snapper, peas 'n rice, plantain, potato salad).
3. Drink it cold for lunch—ice optional, but Uncle Ro will tell you the fridge chill is the point.

Notes: This is about habit, not fancy. Chill the cup while you pack the Sunday plates and drink it cold at lunch. Uncle Ro says the tin can makes it taste like home.

Chapter 18 — The Old Paper Still Talks (Ancient Documents: FRE 803(16))

Sunday dinner ends the same way trials do—somebody wants the last word. The snapper bones are piled up. The peas 'n rice pot is scraped clean. The plantains are down to two lonely slices that nobody claims. And the gossip has turned from loud to surgical.

Auntie Marva goes back to the Bible drawer and pulls out something different this time—an old, folded paper, thin as it is stubborn, dated in ink that has faded into brown. "Y'all want proof?" she says. "I got proof older than everybody in this kitchen."

Nia doesn't even sigh anymore. She just says it: "Hearsay."

Kai leans in. "It can be—unless it fits **FRE 803(16)**, the **ancient documents** exception. If a statement is in a document that's **at least 20 years old** *and* the document is **authentic**, the statement can be admitted even though it's hearsay."

He taps the corner where Auntie wrote the year. "Twenty years is time enough for lies to lose their purpose. But the judge still needs to believe it's real—found where you'd expect, kept the way families keep things, looking like it belongs with the rest of the archive."

Auntie reads a line out loud—an old congratulations note that names the couple, the date, and the church. The kitchen hushes the way it hushes when the old fish comes out crisp: not because everybody agrees, but because everybody recognizes something settled.

- **FRE 803(16):** a statement in a document that is **at least 20 years old** is admissible if the document's **authenticity is established**.
- **Two key moves:** prove the age; prove it's genuine (kept where you'd expect, looks like it belongs, consistent with other evidence).
- **Kitchen translation:** old paper can still talk—but you have to show it's not a fresh fake dressed up as history.

Chapter 19 — The Price Board Is Not Gossip (Market Reports: FRE 803(17))

Next Sunday starts before Sunday—at the fish market, where the snapper is either a blessing or a budget problem. Uncle Ro claims he knows prices by spirit. Tia says, "No you don't. You know prices by memory."

At the counter, there's a printed price sheet and a handwritten board: snapper per pound, plantains by the dozen, limes in a net bag. Not made for court—made so customers can buy without arguing every number.

Kai says, "That's the idea behind **FRE 803(17): market quotations, lists, directories, or other compilations** that are generally relied on by the public or by people in a particular occupation can come in. The rule trusts what the world regularly uses—price lists, published tables, standard directories—because the whole point is accuracy people can rely on."

So when Auntie Marva says, "We can't do four snappers this week—look at the board," she's not repeating gossip. She's pointing to a list the market uses to run its day. But if Ms. Petty scribbles "Snapper cheap today" on a napkin and calls it a 'market report,' that's just her—again—trying to sneak a story in through the side door.

Takeaway Card

- **FRE 803(17):** market quotations, lists, directories, or other compilations generally relied on by the public or by people in a particular occupation.
- **Reliance is the key:** the list is used in the real world to make decisions (prices, availability, standards).
- **Not everything written down qualifies:** a random note is not a relied-on compilation.

Recipe 17

Dish: Fish Market Price-Check (Planning the Signature
Sunday Spread)

Ingredients

- 1 fish market price board/sheet (the one customers
  actually rely on)
- Your Sunday list: red snapper, plantains, limes,
  potatoes, eggs, mayo, mustard, rice, pigeon peas
- A hard budget number (so you don't argue in the aisle)

Method

1. Check snapper price first—because the fish decides the
   whole Sunday mood.
2. Buy plantains and limes no matter what—they stretch
   any plate and save any meal.
3. If snapper is high, adjust the count (or the size), not the
   tradition: keep peas 'n rice, plantain, and potato salad
   steady.
4. Save the receipt (because receipts don't gossip).

Notes: Check snapper price first and let the board tell the
truth. Keep the sides steady (plantain, rice, potato salad) and
adjust fish quantity if needed. Save the receipt.

Chapter 20 — "The Book Said So" (Learned Treatises: FRE 803(18))

The only thing this family respects more than a receipt is a book—an old one, with margins full of notes, the kind that looks like it survived three hurricanes and two aunties.

Auntie Marva is at the stove with the snapper, and Cousin Nia is doing what she does—questioning everything. "Your oil too cold," Nia says. "That fish gon' drink grease."

Tia pulls a book off the shelf like she's pulling rank. "Listen," she says, flipping pages with flour-dusted fingers. "It says right here: keep frying oil hot enough to set the crust quick—so the food doesn't soak. That's why your first batch always tells on you."

Kai nods. "That's **FRE 803(18)—Learned Treatises**. A statement in a treatise, periodical, or pamphlet can be read to the jury if it's called to an expert's attention on cross-examination or relied on by the expert on direct, *and* the publication is established as a reliable authority. The key is the expert: the book comes in through an expert witness, not through kitchen confidence."

He taps the page. "And even then, the rule usually lets the words be **read into evidence**—the jury hears it—but the book itself doesn't go back to the jury room as an exhibit. The law wants the learning, not a library fight in deliberations."

Takeaway Card

- **FRE 803(18):** learned treatises.
- **Gatekeepers:** must be used with an **expert witness** (called to attention on cross or relied on direct).

- **Reliability:** the publication must be established as a **reliable authority** (by expert testimony, admission, or judicial notice).
- **How it comes in:** statements are **read into evidence**; the treatise itself is generally **not** received as an exhibit.

Recipe 18

Dish: Auntie Marva's Fry Guide (For Crisp Snapper &
Plantain)

Ingredients

- 1 heavy skillet or deep pan
- Oil with enough depth to fry (about 1/2 inch for pan-
  frying)
- 1 wooden spoon (Auntie's test tool)
- Optional: kitchen thermometer

Method

1. Heat oil over medium-high until it shimmers. If using a
   thermometer, aim around 350°F–375°F for frying
   snapper.
2. Wooden spoon test: dip the tip into the oil—steady
   bubbles mean it's ready; wild smoking means it's too
   hot.
3. Don't crowd the pan. Crowding drops the temperature
   and turns "crispy" into "greasy."
4. Let the oil come back up between batches—especially if
   you're doing plantains first, snapper last.

Notes: Keep oil hot and don't crowd the pan—temperature is
the difference between crisp and greasy. Let the oil recover
between batches. When the oil is wrong, everybody starts
testifying.

Chapter 21 — "Everybody Know They Married" (Reputation Concerning Family History: FRE 803(19))

After a while, a marriage stops being news and starts being a known thing—the way everybody knows what day Auntie fries fish, and everybody knows Uncle Ro will drink Switcha out that tin can like it's a family crest.

Ms. Petty waves her hand like she's calling witnesses. "Ask anybody at church. Everybody know they married. They sit together, they travel together, they family call him 'son-in-law.' That's not even gossip—that's reputation."

Kai nods. "That's the language of **FRE 803(19): reputation among a person's family, associates, or community** concerning the person's birth, adoption, marriage, divorce, legitimacy, ancestry, relationship by blood or marriage, or similar facts of personal or family history."

He looks at Ms. Petty, gentle but firm. "Reputation isn't 'Ms. Petty heard.' It's what the circle generally believes over time. It's the difference between one spark and a whole neighborhood knowing where the fire always burns."

Takeaway Card

- **FRE 803(19):** reputation among family/associates/community concerning personal or family history (including **marriage**).
- **Scope:** birth, adoption, marriage, divorce, legitimacy, ancestry, relationship by blood or marriage, and similar facts.
- **Distinguish:** community reputation is broader than one person's rumor.

Recipe 19

Dish: After-Church Dessert Table (Coconut Tart + Switcha)

Ingredients

- 1 lattice coconut tart, sliced
- 1 pitcher of Switcha, ice on the side
- Napkins (the tart is worth it, but it will try you)

Method

1. Slice tart and let it sit 10 minutes, so the filling holds together clean.
2. Pour Switcha and chill it hard. Serve ice on the side (so nobody accuses you of watering it down).
3. Save a slice for later—because the next day, somebody will "remember" something new.

Notes: Serve ice on the side so the Switcha stays strong. Let the tart rest a few minutes after slicing so it holds together. Uncle Ro still claims the tin can is colder.

Chapter 22 — "Why Would He Admit That?" (Statement Against Interest: FRE 804(b)(3))

The kitchen gets quiet when Rico's name gets said too many times. Not because anybody's scared—because everybody knows what happens next: somebody will demand the truth from the only person who can give it, and he won't show.

Uncle Ro checks his phone, then checks it again like the screen owes him an answer. "He ain't coming," Ro says. "He told me, 'I'm not talking to nobody about that fish market mess.'"

Nia points with her fork. "So... hearsay. Because Rico's not here, and we're repeating what he said."

Kai nods. "Yes—and that's why **FRE 804** is a whole different section. **These exceptions only open up if the declarant is 'unavailable' under FRE 804(a).**" He ticks them off like ingredients: "Privilege—like pleading the Fifth. Refusing to testify even after a court order. Not remembering. Death or illness. Or being absent and you can't get them here even with reasonable efforts."

Uncle Ro lowers his voice because some words feel like knives even in a kitchen. "Rico told me," Ro says, "'I used that market money to cover something else. I was short. I know I was wrong.'"

Kai nods slowly. "That's the heart of **FRE 804(b)(3)**—a **statement against interest**. If a reasonable person in Rico's position wouldn't have said it unless it were true—because it's so bad for him—then the Rules treat that self-harming quality like a substitute for cross-examination."

The rule covers statements that are against someone's **money** (pecuniary), against their **property rights** (proprietary), or that expose them to **civil or criminal liability**. Rico admitting he misused money is the kind of thing that can cost him—court, reputation, and more. That's why a reasonable person doesn't just say it for fun.

But Kai adds, "Courts listen closely to *what* part is really against interest. 'I was wrong' is against him. 'And the fish market cheated me too' is him trying to spread blame. And when a statement is offered to help someone in a criminal case, the Rules demand **corroborating circumstances** that clearly indicate trustworthiness—because jail-time stories make people creative."

In this family, corroboration looks like Tia's world: the fish market receipts, the missing entry, the catering log, the time-stamps—paper that doesn't care who is embarrassed. If Rico's admission matches the records, it starts sounding less like a performance and more like the truth breaking through.

Takeaway Card

- **Step 1 (Gatekeeper):** FRE 804 exceptions require **unavailability** under **FRE 804(a)** (privilege, refusal, lack of memory, death/illness, or absence despite reasonable efforts).
- **FRE 804(b)(3):** statement a reasonable person would not have made unless true because it was so contrary to the declarant's **pecuniary/proprietary interest** or exposed the declarant to **civil/criminal liability**.
- **Scope:** focus on the truly **self-inculpatory** parts; blame-shifting add-ons are suspect.
- **Trustworthiness:** when required (especially when offered to help the accused), look for **corroborating circumstances** showing reliability.

Recipe 20

Dish: Packing the Sunday Plates (Snapper + Peas 'n Rice + Plantain + Potato Salad)

Ingredients

- Leftover fried snapper (cooled)
- Peas 'n rice
- Fried sweet plantain
- Potato salad (kept cold)
- To-go containers + foil
- Masking tape + marker (Tia's "label everything" rule)

Method

1. Let snapper cool on a rack so it stays as crisp as it can.
2. Pack peas 'n rice while it's still warm (not blazing hot), then seal.
3. Keep potato salad cold—pack it last and put it straight back in the fridge.
4. Label every container with what it is and whose name is on it.

Notes: Cool snapper on a rack so it stays crisp. Keep potato salad cold and separate. Labeling containers stops "I never got a plate" arguments before they start.

Chapter 23 — The Gossip Layer Cake (Hearsay Within Hearsay: FRE 805)

By the time the Sunday plates are packed and labeled, the kitchen has one job left: retell the day. That's when the gossip turns into a dessert—sweet, heavy, and layered.

Ms. Petty comes back in the doorway like she forgot something on purpose. "I just talked to Pastor Dean," she says. "And Pastor Dean said Rico told him, 'Tell them I admit I used the fish-market money—and I'm not paying it back.'"

Nia almost smiles. "That's not just hearsay. That's hearsay wearing hearsay like a wig."

Kai nods. "Exactly. **FRE 805** calls it **hearsay within hearsay**. The rule is blunt: a layered statement is admissible only if **each part** of the combined statement fits an exception or exclusion. One clean layer can't save a dirty one."

He points at the sentence like it's a recipe card. "We've got layers: (1) Ms. Petty repeating what (2) Pastor Dean allegedly said about what (3) Rico allegedly said. If this is offered for its truth—'Rico admitted it'—then every step in that chain needs a rule that lets it in."

Uncle Ro leans forward. "So how we get it in?"

"First," Kai says, "you can *peel layers off*. If Pastor Dean testifies, you don't need Ms. Petty to repeat him. And if Tia has Rico's own voice note or text, you don't need Pastor Dean repeating Rico."

He taps the counter. "Rico's own words, offered against Rico, are **not hearsay** under **FRE 801(d)(2)(A)**. If Rico is unavailable and the statement truly hurts him—money, liability—that's where **FRE**

804(b)(3) can also come up. But Ms. Petty repeating Pastor Dean repeating Rico is the hardest way to prove the same point."

Kai keeps going because the kitchen always gives you more than one example. "Say Tia tells the court, 'The receipt says Rico bought four snappers.' That can be two layers too: Tia's statement about what the receipt says, and the receipt itself. You can fix it by admitting the **receipt as a business record** under **FRE 803(6)** (with proper foundation). Or better—just offer the receipt and let Tia authenticate it, instead of offering Tia's paraphrase for its truth."

"Or take the marriage talk," Kai says, waving a hand toward the dessert table. "Auntie reads the Bible entry (**FRE 803(13)**), and Ms. Petty adds, 'Everybody at church knows they've been married for years' (**FRE 803(19)**). If you try to stack it wrong—like 'Ms. Petty said her cousin said the clerk said they're married'—and one layer has no rule to support it, the whole statement collapses. That's FRE 805: one bad layer spoils the whole plate."

Takeaway Card

- **FRE 805:** hearsay within hearsay is admissible only if **each layer** fits a hearsay exclusion/exception.
- **Step 1:** break the quote into layers (who said what to whom).
- **Step 2:** assign a rule to **each** layer (e.g., 801(d)(2), 803(6), 803(13), 804(b)(3)).
- **Fix strategy:** "peel layers off" by calling the closer witness or offering the original record/recording instead of someone's paraphrase.
- **If one layer fails,** the whole combined statement fails (even if the other layers are admissible).

Recipe 21

Dish: Warm Coconut Syrup (For Lattice Coconut Tart Slices)

Ingredients

- 1/2 cup canned coconut milk
- 2 tbsp sugar
- 1 tbsp butter
- 1/2 tsp vanilla
- Pinch of salt

Method

1. In a small saucepan over low heat, warm coconut milk, sugar, butter, and salt until melted and smooth.
2. Stir in vanilla and warm 30 seconds more.
3. Spoon lightly over tart slices right before serving.

Notes: Spoon lightly—this is a finish, not a soak. Keep the heat low so it stays smooth. Best served warm over tart slices.

Right when you think the kitchen is winding down, somebody always comes through the door with a foil pan and a grin— because in this family, evidence isn't the only thing that shows up late. So does the mac, and so does the mischief.

Recipe 22

Dish: Bahamian Baked Macaroni

Ingredients

- 1 lb. elbow macaroni
- 2 tbsp butter (for greasing the pan)
- 3 large eggs
- 1 (12 oz) can evaporated milk
- 1/2 cup whole milk (or more evaporated milk)
- 1 tsp kosher salt (to taste)
- 1 onion diced
- 1 bell pepper diced
- 1 stalk of celery diced
- 1/2 tsp black pepper
- 1/2 tsp paprika
- 1/4 tsp cayenne (optional)
- 1 lb. cheddar cheese, grated (about 4 cups), divided

Method

1. Preheat oven to 350°F. Grease a 9x13-inch baking dish with butter.
2. Boil macaroni in salted water until just tender. Drain well.
3. In a large bowl, whisk eggs, evaporated milk, milk, salt, pepper, onion, celery, bell pepper, paprika (and cayenne if using).
4. Stir macaroni into the egg mixture. Fold in about 3 cups of the grated cheddar
5. Pour into the baking dish. Top with remaining cheese.
6. Bake 35–45 minutes, until set and browned on top. Rest 10 minutes before cutting.

Notes: This mac is meant to slice—let it rest 10 minutes before cutting. Don't overboil the pasta before baking.

Recipe 23

Dish: Virgin Bahamian Sky Juice

Ingredients

- 2 cups coconut water (chilled)
- 1/2 cup sweetened condensed milk (adjust to taste)
- 2 tbsp fresh lime juice (optional but brightens it)
- Ice
- Optional: pinch of grated nutmeg or cinnamon on top

Method

1. Fill a pitcher with ice.
2. Pour in coconut water, condensed milk, and lime juice (if using). Stir well until fully combined.
3. Taste and adjust: more condensed milk for sweeter/creamier, more coconut water for lighter.
4. Pour into cups over ice. Dust with a pinch of nutmeg if you like.

Notes: Stir well so the condensed milk fully blends. Taste and adjust for your crowd (sweeter vs lighter).

Chapter 24 — Last Resort, Best Story (Residual Exception: FRE 807)

The foil pan hits the counter like a gavel.

"Y'all thought we was done?" Cousin Nia's sister—Kayla, the one who shows love in aluminum trays—slides in with Bahamian baked macaroni, browned on top and cut to slice, smelling like sharp cheddar and Sunday pride. The snapper is already gone, but the mac makes the room rearrange itself anyway.

Right behind her comes Uncle Ro with a pitcher that looks like trouble wearing ice. "Sky Juice," he announces, setting it right beside the Switcha like he's daring anybody to choose peace. Auntie Marva doesn't reach for it, but her eyes cut to it— quick—like memory has a taste.

And that's when Ms. Petty—powered by sugar, coconut, and attention—drops a sentence that would make a trial lawyer sit up straight. "I'm telling you," she says, "I heard it from somebody who was *there*: Rico admitted he took the money, and he said he did it because he knew nobody would press him."

Nia points her fork like a citation. "Objection. Hearsay within hearsay. And don't look at me like it's excited utterance either—Ms. Petty is always excited."

Kai nods, chewing like he's thinking. "Most of the time, the Rules want you to use the named pathways—801, 803, 804. But sometimes you have a statement that feels unusually reliable and unusually necessary, and there's no perfect label for it. That's when people whisper about **FRE 807**—the **residual exception**. It's the 'last resort' door, and judges don't leave it wide open."

Under **FRE 807**, a hearsay statement may come in if: (1) it has **equivalent circumstantial guarantees of trustworthiness**; (2) it's offered as evidence of a **material fact**; (3) it's **more probative** on that point than any other evidence you can reasonably get; and (4) admitting it will best serve the **purposes of the Rules** and the **interests of justice**. Plus—like Tia always reminds everybody—there's a **notice requirement**: you don't ambush the other side with surprise hearsay.

Uncle Ro tilts the Sky Juice pitcher like he's weighing it. "So the judge just lets in whatever sound good?"

"No," Kai says. "If you can get the fish market records, you get them. If you can get Rico's own text, you use **801(d)(2)**. If you can call the person who was 'there,' you call them. **FRE 807 is not a shortcut.** It's baked macaroni at the end—brought out when the table is already full and you still need that one last thing to make the meal make sense."

Auntie Marva finally speaks, eyes still on the drink. "Trust is everything," she says. "Same way I don't take just any sip, I don't take just any story." Then she reaches for the mac instead—safe choice, solid proof, sliced clean.

Takeaway Card

- **FRE 807:** the residual exception—narrow, judge-controlled, and not a first choice.
- **Must show:** (1) strong guarantees of trustworthiness; (2) material fact; (3) more probative than other reasonably available evidence; (4) interests of justice/purposes of the Rules.
- **Notice:** you must give the other side advance notice and details of the statement.
- **Practical instinct:** if another rule fits (801/803/804), use it—807 is for the rare leftover problem.

Chapter 25 — "Everybody Know Where That Line Is" (Boundaries & General History: FRE 803(20))

Right after the dessert table, the family drifts outside like the conversation needs fresh air. And that's when "everybody knows" changes categories. Inside, it's marriage talk. Outside, it's land talk.

Ms. Petty points across the yard with a certainty only rumor can buy. "That mango tree been the line since I was little. Everybody know that fence ain't the line—the tree is the line."

Kai nods. "That's **FRE 803(20): reputation in a community** about **boundaries** of land, customs that affect land, or other matters of general history important to the community. The rule is basically admitting that some facts live in the neighborhood's long memory, not in one person's mouth."

Takeaway Card

- **FRE 803(20):** reputation in a community concerning boundaries of land, customs affecting land, or other matters of general history important to the community.
- **Think:** "everybody knows where the line is" facts—built over time, not made for court.
- **Watch the proof:** it must be community reputation, not one person's fresh rumor.

Chapter 26 — Reputation Ain't a Screenshot (Character: FRE 803(21))

Back inside, the conversation slides from what happened to who somebody *is*. That's always where Sunday gets dangerous.

Ms. Petty says, "Everybody know Rico don't pay on time. That's his character." Nia cuts her eyes: "That's your opinion."

Kai nods. "There's a hearsay exception for that kind of 'everybody knows' too: **FRE 803(21)—reputation among a person's associates or in the community concerning the person's character**. It's not about one story. It's about the long-running reputation people share. (Whether character evidence is allowed for the purpose you want is a separate Evidence question—but this rule addresses the hearsay problem when reputation is the proof.)

Takeaway Card

- **FRE 803(21):** reputation among a person's associates or in the community concerning the person's character.
- **Key idea:** reputation is bigger than one incident; it's the community's shared view over time.
- **Reminder:** this solves the hearsay issue—separate rules control when character evidence is relevant/admissible.

Chapter 27 — "The Judgment Is the Receipt" (Previous Conviction: FRE 803(22))

Uncle Ro says, "Y'all keep arguing like the court don't keep records." Tia nods. "Judgments are paper too."

Kai nods. "**FRE 803(22)** covers a **judgment of a previous conviction**. A final judgment—after trial or guilty plea—can be admitted to prove **any fact essential to the judgment**, especially when the conviction was for a crime punishable by death or imprisonment for more than one year. Like everything else, it's not a free-for-all, but the rule treats the judgment itself like a reliable record of what the court decided."

Takeaway Card

- **FRE 803(22):** evidence of a final judgment of conviction can be admissible to prove a fact essential to that judgment.
- **Typical trigger:** felony-level conviction (punishable by > 1 year) after trial or guilty plea.
- **Limit:** the judgment proves facts essential to the judgment, not every rumor around the case.

Chapter 28 — Old Judgments, Old Truths (Personal/Family/General History: FRE 803(23))

Auntie Marva says, "Sometimes the only honest record left is an old court paper. People die. Stories change. But judgments sit."

Kai nods. "That's **FRE 803(23)**. Some judgments are admitted to prove matters of **personal, family, or general history**—or boundaries—when those matters were essential to the judgment. It's another way the Rules recognize that long-running facts sometimes get settled on paper in a courtroom, and that paper can later be used to prove what was settled."

Takeaway Card

- **FRE 803(23):** judgments may be admissible to prove matters of personal, family, or general history (or boundaries) when those matters were essential to the judgment.
- **Use:** when the judgment itself is the best surviving proof of a settled historical fact.

Wrap-Up — The Sunday Dinner Method (Putting FRE 801–807 Together)

By now you've seen what this family already knew: the kitchen is a courtroom long before anybody says "objection." When the oil is hot and the stories are hotter, you don't win by talking the loudest—you win by asking the right questions in the right order.

Wrap-Up Summary

The Wrap-Up chapter gives you a single repeatable workflow for every hearsay problem: define the statement (FRE 801(a)), identify whether it's offered for truth (FRE 801(c)), and remember the default rule of exclusion (FRE 802). From there, you move in order—first checking the "not hearsay" categories (FRE 801(d)(1) and (2)), then the broad 803 exceptions (where availability doesn't matter), then the 804 exceptions (only if the declarant is unavailable). Before you celebrate, you check whether you're dealing with stacked gossip (FRE 805), because every layer needs its own rule. And if nothing fits, you only then consider the narrow last-resort door (FRE 807), with its trustworthiness and notice requirements. In other words: the Sunday Dinner Method keeps your analysis as clean as a well-run kitchen—step-by-step, no skipping, no guessing.

So here is the Sunday Dinner Method—the flow you run every time somebody tries to slide a statement across the table like seasoning.

1. **Identify the "statement" (FRE 801(a)):** Is it oral, written, or conduct meant as an assertion?
2. **Ask the purpose:** Why is it being offered? If it's not for truth (effect on listener, notice, verbal act,

impeachment, context), it's often **not hearsay** (FRE 801(c)).

3. **If it is for truth:** it's hearsay and starts excluded (FRE 802) unless a rule saves it.
4. **Check "not hearsay" categories (FRE 801(d)):** prior statements by a testifying witness (801(d)(1)) and opposing party statements (801(d)(2)).
5. **Check FRE 803 exceptions (availability doesn't matter):** present sense impression, excited utterance, state of mind, medical treatment, recorded recollection, business records, public records, family records, market reports, learned treatises, reputation, and more.
6. **If FRE 803 doesn't fit, ask: is the declarant unavailable (FRE 804(a))?** If yes, consider FRE 804 exceptions, including **statement against interest** (804(b)(3)).
7. **Always check for layers (FRE 805):** if the statement is stacked ("he said she said"), every layer needs its own rule.
8. **Only then consider the last door (FRE 807):** the residual exception—rare, reliability-heavy, and notice-required.

The signature spread keeps you honest. Snapper needs hot oil. Rice needs time. Potato salad needs chill. And hearsay needs structure. If you follow the order, you won't confuse yourself: you'll know when a statement is just gossip, when it's admissible truth, and when it's a layered mess that collapses the moment you look at it too hard.

Final Takeaway Card (One-Page Checklist)

- **Purpose?** (truth vs. not-for-truth)
- **Declarant available?** (matters for 804, not for 803)
- **801(d) not hearsay?** (prior statements / opposing party statements)
- **803 exception?** (timing, routine, reliability)
- **804 exception?** (unavailability + special reliability)
- **805 layers?** (every layer covered)

- **807 last resort?** (trustworthy, necessary, notice)

- **807 last resort?** (trustworthy, necessary, notice)

Glossary of Key FRE & Evidence Terms

Term	Plain-English Meaning
Assertion	A claim that something is true. Nonverbal conduct counts only if intended as an assertion. (FRE 801(a))
Statement	Oral, written, or nonverbal conduct intended as an assertion. (FRE 801(a))
Declarant	The person who made the statement.
Hearsay	An out-of-court statement offered to prove the truth of what it asserts. (FRE 801(c))
Truth of the matter asserted	Using the statement because you want the fact in the statement to be believed as true.
Not-for-truth purpose	Using words for another reason (effect on listener, notice, verbal acts, impeachment, context), so it may be non-hearsay.

Default hearsay rule	Hearsay is inadmissible unless a federal statute, the FRE, or other rules provide otherwise. (FRE 802)
Prior statement (witness)	Certain prior statements by a witness are treated as not hearsay if the declarant testifies and is subject to cross. (FRE 801(d)(1))
Opposing party statement	Certain statements offered against an opposing party are not hearsay: party's own statement, adoptive, authorized, agent/employee, co-conspirator. (FRE 801(d)(2))
Present sense impression	Description/explanation of an event made while perceiving it or immediately after. (FRE 803(1))
Excited utterance	Statement relating to a startling event made while still under the stress of excitement. (FRE 803(2))
Then-existing state of mind	Statements of current intent, motive, plan, or emotional/physical condition; not memory/belief to prove past facts (with limited exceptions). (FRE 803(3))
Medical diagnosis/treatment	Statements made for and reasonably pertinent to diagnosis/treatment (symptoms, pain, cause). (FRE 803(4))

Recorded recollection	If witness once knew but can't recall well enough now, a record made/adopted when fresh and accurate may be read into evidence. (FRE 803(5))
Business records	Records of regularly conducted activity with proper foundation; can be excluded if untrustworthy. (FRE 803(6))
Absence of business record	Using a missing entry to prove something did not occur or does not exist where it normally would be recorded. (FRE 803(7))
Public records	Records of a public office's activities, observations, or factual findings (subject to trustworthiness and limits). (FRE 803(8))
Vital statistics	Birth, death, and marriage records reported to a public office under a legal duty. (FRE 803(9))
Absence of public record	A diligent search finds no record where one would exist. (FRE 803(10))
Family records	Family-maintained records about personal/family history (e.g., family Bible). (FRE 803(13))

Property record	Record of a document affecting an interest in property (recorded deed/mortgage/lien) offered to prove its contents. (FRE 803(14))
Statements in property documents	Statements in deeds/leases/etc. relevant to the property interest, supported by later consistent dealings. (FRE 803(15))
Ancient documents	Statements in authentic documents at least 20 years old. (FRE 803(16))
Market reports / commercial publications	Lists/quotations/directories generally relied upon by the public or a trade. (FRE 803(17))
Learned treatise	Reliable authority (treatise/periodical/pamphlet) used with an expert; read into evidence, not typically admitted as an exhibit. (FRE 803(18))
Reputation (family history)	Reputation among family/associates/community concerning personal or family history (including marriage). (FRE 803(19))
Unavailability	Declarant can't be brought to testify for reasons listed in the rules (privilege, refusal, lack of memory, death/illness, absence despite reasonable efforts). (FRE 804(a))

Statement against interest	Unavailable declarant's statement so contrary to their interest (money/property/liability) that a reasonable person wouldn't say it unless true; may require corroboration for trustworthiness in certain situations. (FRE 804(b)(3))
Hearsay within hearsay	Layered statements ("he said she said"); admissible only if each layer is independently covered. (FRE 805)
Residual exception	Last-resort hearsay exception requiring strong trustworthiness, materiality, necessity, interests of justice, and notice. (FRE 807)

Flashcards (From the Glossary)

Term	Cover and test your knowledge
Assertion	A claim that something is true; nonverbal conduct counts only if intended as an assertion. (FRE 801(a))
Statement	Oral, written, or nonverbal conduct intended as an assertion. (FRE 801(a))
Declarant	The person who made the statement.
Hearsay	Out-of-court statement offered to prove the truth of what it asserts. (FRE 801(c))
Truth of the matter asserted	Using the statement because you want the fact inside it to be believed as true.
Not-for-truth purpose	Using the words for something other than truth (effect on listener, notice, verbal act, impeachment, context) so it may be non-hearsay.
Default hearsay rule	Hearsay is inadmissible unless a rule/statute allows it. (FRE 802)
Prior statement (witness)	Certain prior statements are not hearsay if declarant testifies and is subject to cross. (FRE 801(d)(1))

Opposing party statement	Certain statements offered against an opposing party are not hearsay. (FRE 801(d)(2))
Present sense impression	Description/explanation of an event made while perceiving it or immediately after. (FRE 803(1))
Excited utterance	Statement relating to a startling event made while still under stress/excitement. (FRE 803(2))
Then-existing state of mind	Statements of current intent/motive/plan or emotional/physical condition; not memory/belief to prove past facts. (FRE 803(3))
Medical diagnosis/treatment	Statements made for and reasonably pertinent to diagnosis/treatment (symptoms, pain, cause). (FRE 803(4))
Recorded recollection	Record made/adopted when fresh and accurate may be read into evidence when witness can't recall well enough now. (FRE 803(5))

Business records	Records of regularly conducted activity admitted with foundation; may be excluded if untrustworthy. (FRE 803(6))
Absence of business record	Missing entry can prove nonoccurrence/nonexistence if it would normally be recorded. (FRE 803(7))
Public records	Records of a public office's activities/observations/findings (subject to trustworthiness limits). (FRE 803(8))
Vital statistics	Birth/death/marriage records reported to a public office under a legal duty. (FRE 803(9))
Absence of public record	A diligent search finds no record where one would exist. (FRE 803(10))
Family records	Family-maintained records about personal/family history (e.g., family Bible). (FRE 803(13))

Property record	Record of a recorded property document (deed/mortgage/lien) offered to prove its contents. (FRE 803(14))
Statements in property documents	Statements in deeds/leases/etc. relevant to property interest, supported by later consistent dealings. (FRE 803(15))
Ancient documents	Statements in authentic documents at least 20 years old. (FRE 803(16))
Market reports / commercial publications	Market quotations/lists/directories/compilations generally relied on by public or a trade. (FRE 803(17))
Learned treatise	Reliable authority used with an expert; statement read into evidence; treatise not typically an exhibit. (FRE 803(18))
Reputation (family history)	Reputation among family/associates/community concerning family history (incl. marriage). (FRE 803(19))
Unavailability	Declarant can't testify due to privilege/refusal/no memory/death/illness/absence despite reasonable efforts. (FRE 804(a))

Statement against interest	Unavailable declarant's self-damaging statement (money/property/liability) that a reasonable person wouldn't make unless true. (FRE 804(b)(3))
Hearsay within hearsay	Layered statement admissible only if each layer fits a rule. (FRE 805)
Residual exception	Last-resort hearsay exception: trustworthy + material + necessary + justice + notice. (FRE 807)

Study Quiz (Based on the Chapters)

Answer without overthinking: (1) Is it offered for truth? (2) If yes, what rule lets it in (if any)? If it's layered, name the rule for each layer. Then check the Answer Key.

1. **Define:** Under FRE 801(c), what two things must be true for a statement to be hearsay?
2. **Purpose check:** A witness testifies, "I heard Auntie Marva say, 'The oil is too hot!' and that's why I turned the burner down." Is the statement offered for its truth, and is it hearsay?
3. **FRE 801(d)(2):** Ms. Petty testifies, "Rico texted me, 'I'm not paying them.'" If offered against Rico, is it hearsay? Name the subpart.
4. **Adoptive admission:** Rico is accused at the table ("You stiffed them!"). He hears it and stays silent. What FRE 801(d)(2) theory might apply, and what key circumstance must be present?
5. **Present sense impression:** Little Jalen blurts, "The snapper is sticking to the pan!" as he watches it happen. What rule might admit the statement, and what timing requirement matters most?
6. **Excited utterance:** Hot oil pops and someone yells, "Nia pushed me!" What rule might apply, and what is the core reliability idea?
7. **State of mind limit:** Auntie says, "I'm not sitting by Rico because he threatened me last week." Under FRE 803(3), which part is most likely admissible, and which part is the hearsay problem?
8. **Medical treatment:** At urgent care, Jalen tells the nurse, "Hot oil splashed my hand when the pan tipped." What rule applies, and why does the law trust it?
9. **Recorded recollection:** Auntie Marva can't remember exact measurements, but she wrote them down that day and says the note is accurate. What rule applies, and how does the record come into evidence?
10. **Business records:** Tia offers a fish market receipt showing "2 red snappers" purchased. List two foundation elements required by FRE 803(6).

11. **Absence of business record:** Tia testifies, "There is no receipt showing Rico paid last week." What rule covers this kind of proof, and what must be shown about the recordkeeping system?
12. **Public records:** A government inspection report is offered to show the fish market's score. What rule applies, and what is the big limitation concept that can still keep it out?
13. **Vital statistics:** A certified marriage record is offered to prove two people are married. What rule is this (number and name)?
14. **No record found:** A clerk's letter says a diligent search found no marriage record for the couple. What rule is this (number and name)?
15. **Family record:** A family Bible page lists "Married: ____ / ____." What rule might admit it?
16. **Ancient documents:** Auntie produces an authentic, dated paper that is 25 years old. What rule might admit statements in it?
17. **Market reports:** A fish market price board is offered to show snapper prices that week. What rule might admit it, and what "reliance" idea is key?
18. **Unavailability gate:** Before you can use FRE 804(b)(3), what must be true about the declarant under FRE 804(a)?
19. **Statement against interest:** Rico (unavailable) told Uncle Ro, "I used the money; I was short." What rule applies, and what part of the statement is most trustworthy?
20. **Hearsay within hearsay:** Ms. Petty testifies, "Pastor Dean said Rico said, 'I admit it.'" Under FRE 805, what must you do to admit this?

Answer Key (Study Quiz)

1. It must be (1) an out-of-court statement, and (2) offered to prove the truth of what it asserts.
2. Not offered for truth (it's offered to show effect on listener/why the witness acted). Not hearsay.
3. Not hearsay under FRE 801(d)(2)(A) (opposing party's own statement).
4. FRE 801(d)(2)(B) adoptive admission. Circumstances must be such that a reasonable person would have denied the accusation if untrue.
5. FRE 803(1) present sense impression. Must be made while perceiving the event or immediately after.
6. FRE 803(2) excited utterance. Reliability comes from stress/excitement limiting reflection/fabrication.
7. "I'm not sitting by Rico" (then-existing state of mind) is most likely admissible; "because he threatened me last week" is generally a memory/past fact offered for truth and is the problem.
8. FRE 803(4). The law trusts it because people seeking diagnosis/treatment have a strong motive to be truthful about symptoms and cause.
9. FRE 803(5). The record is read into evidence (not automatically received as an exhibit unless the adverse party offers it).
10. Any two: made at/near the time; by someone with knowledge; kept in the course of regularly conducted activity; making it was a regular practice; shown by custodian/qualified witness; trustworthy.
11. FRE 803(7). Must show the system regularly keeps such records and the matter would normally be recorded; the absence is meaningful.
12. FRE 803(8) public records. It can still be excluded if circumstances indicate lack of trustworthiness (and certain law-enforcement limits may apply in criminal cases).
13. FRE 803(9) public records of vital statistics.
14. FRE 803(10) absence of a public record (no record found after diligent search).

15. FRE 803(13) family records.
16. FRE 803(16) ancient documents (20+ years old and
    authentic).
17. FRE 803(17). Key idea: the list/quotation is generally
    relied on by the public or the trade.
18. Declarant must be "unavailable" as defined by FRE
    804(a) (e.g., privilege/refusal/death/illness/absence
    despite reasonable efforts).
19. FRE 804(b)(3) statement against interest. The most
    trustworthy part is the truly self-inculpatory admission
    ("I used the money; I was short"), not blame-shifting
    extras.
20. Break into layers and supply a rule for each layer (e.g.,
    get Rico's statement in via 801(d)(2)(A) or 804(b)(3),
    and cover the Pastor Dean/Ms. Petty layer by calling the
    witness or another applicable rule). If any layer lacks a
    rule, the combined statement is inadmissible.

One-Page Attack Outline (Hearsay)

Goal: In 60–120 seconds, classify the statement (not hearsay vs hearsay), then pick the cleanest admission path (801(d) → 803 → 804), check layers (805), and only then consider 807.

1. **Identify the evidence:** What exact words/act are being offered? Who is the declarant? (FRE 801(a))
2. **Purpose question:** Is it offered for the truth of what it asserts? (FRE 801(c))
   - If **not** for truth: likely **not hearsay** (effect on listener, notice/knowledge, verbal act, impeachment, context).
3. **If for truth:** hearsay → excluded by default. (FRE 802)
4. **Check "Not Hearsay" categories first:**
   - **801(d)(1)** Prior statements (declarant testifies + subject to cross): (A) inconsistent under oath; (B) consistent to rebut fabrication/improper motive (timing matters); (C) prior ID.
   - **801(d)(2)** Opposing party statements (offered against party): (A) own statement; (B) adoptive; (C) authorized; (D) agent/employee within scope + during; (E) co-conspirator during + in furtherance (with foundation).
5. **Then check FRE 803 exceptions (availability irrelevant):**
   - **Timing** exceptions: 803(1) present sense; 803(2) excited utterance.
   - **Mind/body**: 803(3) then-existing state of mind (no past-fact smuggling); 803(4) medical diagnosis/treatment.
   - **Records**: 803(5) recorded recollection (read in); 803(6) business records; 803(7) absence of record; 803(8) public records; 803(9) vital stats; 803(10) no public record found; 803(13) family records; 803(14)–(15) property records; 803(16) ancient docs; 803(17) market reports; 803(18) learned treatises (expert + read in); 803(19) reputation family history.

6. **If no 803 fits, ask about unavailability:** Is the declarant unavailable under FRE 804(a) (privilege/refusal/no memory/death or illness/absence despite reasonable efforts)?
7. **If unavailable, check FRE 804 exceptions:** (in this book: **804(b)(3)** statement against interest—use only the truly self-inculpatory parts; look for corroboration/trustworthiness when required).
8. **Always run FRE 805:** If there are layers ("X said Y said…"), assign a rule to **each layer**. If one layer fails, the whole combined statement fails.
9. **Last door only (FRE 807):** residual exception—strong trustworthiness + material fact + more probative than other reasonably available evidence + interests of justice + notice.
10. **Write it clean:** "Offered for truth → hearsay (801(c), 802) → admissible under [rule] because [elements]," and if layered, repeat per layer.

Study Guide (Key Points & Exam Traps)

Use this as your quick review after reading the stories. It's the same "Sunday Dinner Method," organized by rule family, with the most testable elements and the most common places students get tricked.

FRE 801–802 Foundations

- **Start with purpose (FRE 801(c)):** Ask, "Why are we offering these words?" If it's not for truth (effect on listener, notice, verbal act, impeachment, context), it's often not hearsay.
- **Define the statement (FRE 801(a)):** oral/written, plus nonverbal conduct only if intended as an assertion.
- **Default rule (FRE 802):** if it is hearsay, it's out unless a rule lets it in.

FRE 801(d) "Not Hearsay" Categories (High Yield)

- **801(d)(1) Prior statements:** declarant must **testify** and be **subject to cross**. (A) inconsistent statement must be **under oath** at trial/hearing/deposition; (B) consistent statement must fit the rehab purpose and timing; (C) prior identification after perceiving.
- **801(d)(2) Opposing party statements:** offered **against** the party. Know (A) party's own words; (B) adoptive; (C) authorized; (D) agent/employee within scope and during relationship; (E) co-conspirator during and in furtherance (with foundation).
- **Trap:** students call these "exceptions," but the FRE labels them **not hearsay.**

FRE 803 Exceptions (Availability Doesn't Matter)

- **803(1) Present sense impression:** timing is everything—"while perceiving or immediately after." Too much delay = too much story.
- **803(2) Excited utterance:** look for a startling event + continuing stress; the calmer the declarant, the weaker the fit.
- **803(3) State of mind:** present intent/motive/plan fits; don't smuggle past facts ("because he did X last week").
- **803(4) Medical diagnosis/treatment:** symptoms + cause that a medical professional would reasonably need; blame/identity usually not pertinent.
- **803(5) Recorded recollection:** witness can't recall well enough now; record made/adopted when fresh and accurate; read into evidence (not automatically an exhibit).
- **803(6) Business records:** routine, near-time, knowledge, regular practice + custodian/qualified witness; watch the trustworthiness "escape hatch."
- **803(7) Absence of record:** must show the system would normally record it; missing entry matters only if the system is reliable.
- **803(8) Public records:** public office activities/observations/findings; trustworthiness can still exclude; remember special limits in certain criminal contexts.
- **803(9)–(10) Vital stats / no record found:** marriage records (or diligent search showing none) beat kitchen rumor.
- **803(13) Family records:** family Bible/genealogy type records about family history.
- **803(14)–(15) Property records:** recorded deed records (14) and statements inside property documents (15) supported by later consistent dealings.
- **803(16) Ancient documents:** 20+ years + authenticity—age alone isn't enough.

- **803(17) Market reports:** relied-on price boards/lists, not random notes.
- **803(18) Learned treatises:** requires an expert; reliable authority; read into evidence; not typically an exhibit.
- **803(19) Reputation (family history):** community reputation over time, not one person's rumor.

FRE 804, 805, 807 (When the Kitchen Gets Complicated)

- **804(a) Gatekeeper:** you don't get 804 exceptions unless you can show **unavailability** (privilege/refusal/no memory/death or illness/absence despite reasonable efforts).
- **804(b)(3) Statement against interest:** focus on the truly self-inculpatory part; watch for blame-shifting; when required, look for corroboration/trustworthiness indicators.
- **805 Layers:** break the statement into links in the chain—every link needs its own rule; "peel layers" by getting closer to the source or offering the original record/recording.
- **807 Residual:** last door only—trustworthy + material + more probative than other obtainable evidence + interests of justice + notice.

Quick Issue-Spotting Prompts

- Who is the declarant, and are they in court?
- What fact is the proponent trying to prove with the statement?
- Is the statement a description of a moment (803(1)), a stress-blurt (803(2)), a present plan/feeling (803(3)), or a medical explanation (803(4))?
- Is there a record (receipt, notebook, report) that is better than somebody's retelling (803(5), 803(6), 803(8))?
- Is the statement offered against the opponent (801(d)(2))?
- Is it layered ("X said Y said...")? If yes, do 805 immediately.

Chapter-by-Chapter Summary (Quick Review)

1. **Chapter 1 (FRE 801(a), 801(c)):** Defines hearsay and shows the first move—purpose—by contrasting truth-use gossip with not-for-truth kitchen talk (notice/effect/context).
2. **Chapter 2 (Why hearsay is excluded):** Explains the "why" (cross-exam and the perception/memory/sincerity/narration risks) that drives the rule and its exceptions.
3. **Chapter 3 (FRE 801(d)(2)):** The juicy opponent-mouth chapter—party statements, adoptive admissions, authorized/agent statements, and co-conspirator talk, all in one family argument.
4. **Chapter 4 (FRE 801(d)(1)):** Prior statements come alive—when the witness is on the stand now, certain earlier versions (inconsistent/consistent/ID) can come in for their truth.
5. **Chapter 5 (FRE 803(1)):** Present sense impressions—real-time "oil is hot" statements made during or immediately after the event.
6. **Chapter 6 (FRE 803(2)):** Excited utterances—truth under stress, when the grease pops and the words come out before the filter.
7. **Chapter 7 (FRE 803(3)):** State of mind—"I'm not sitting by him"—and the key limitation against using memory/belief to prove past facts.
8. **Chapter 8 (FRE 803(4)):** Medical statements—what you tell the nurse about symptoms and cause (not blame) and why the Rules trust it.
9. **Chapter 9 (FRE 803(5)):** Auntie's notebook becomes recorded recollection—when memory fails, a fresh, accurate record can be read into evidence.
10. **Chapter 10 (FRE 803(6)):** Receipts and catering invoices teach business records—routine, near-time records with foundation, plus the trustworthiness escape hatch.

11. **Chapter 11 (FRE 803(7)):** The missing receipt teaches absence of a record—silence can prove nonoccurrence if the system would normally record it.
12. **Chapter 12 (FRE 803(8)):** The inspector's paperwork teaches public records and the continuing role of trustworthiness limits.
13. **Chapter 13 (FRE 803(9)–(10)):** A marriage announcement leads to vital statistics records (and "no record found") as proof stronger than rumor.
14. **Chapter 14 (FRE 803(11)–(12)):** Certified records show how paperwork can substitute for a live custodian witness when proper notice and certification exist.
15. **Chapter 15 (FRE 803(13)):** Family Bible and family archives teach family records—kept to remember life, not to win lawsuits.
16. **Chapter 16 (FRE 803(14)):** A deed record teaches property-records admissibility—recorded documents affecting property can prove their contents.
17. **Chapter 17 (FRE 803(15)):** The deed's own language teaches statements in property documents, supported by later consistent dealings.
18. **Chapter 18 (FRE 803(16)):** Old papers from the Bible drawer teach ancient documents—20+ years plus authenticity.
19. **Chapter 19 (FRE 803(17)):** Fish market price boards teach market reports—compilations the public/trade actually relies on.
20. **Chapter 20 (FRE 803(18)):** The book on the shelf teaches learned treatises—expert gatekeeping, reliable authority, read-in (not exhibit).
21. **Chapter 21 (FRE 803(19)):** Church/community "everybody knows" teaches reputation concerning personal or family history.
22. **Chapter 22 (FRE 804(a), 804(b)(3)):** Rico's absence opens FRE 804 and the statement-against-interest exception—self-inculpatory parts plus corroboration/trustworthiness.
23. **Chapter 23 (FRE 805):** The layered gossip chapter—every layer needs its own exception or exclusion, or the whole cake falls.

24. **Chapter 24 (FRE 807):** Baked macaroni and Sky Juice set the stage for the residual exception—last resort, reliability-heavy, and notice-required.
25. **Wrap-Up (FRE 801–807):** Pulls the entire book into one repeatable workflow ("Sunday Dinner Method") plus a one-page checklist for exam writing.

Index (Quick Topic Lookup)

Additional Recipes (For the Next Sunday)

Recipe — Bahamian Boiled Fish (Grouper)

Dish: Boiled Fish (Grouper) with Lime & Peppers

Ingredients

- 2 lb. grouper (steaks or large chunks)
- 8 cups water
- 1 tbsp kosher salt (plus more to taste)
- 1 medium onion, sliced
- 1 green bell pepper, sliced
- 2 cloves garlic, smashed
- 2 medium potatoes, peeled and chunked (optional but common)
- 1 tsp dried thyme
- 1–2 small hot peppers (goat pepper or habanero), whole (do not burst)
- 2 tbsp tomato paste (optional, for a richer broth)
- Juice of 2 limes (plus wedges to serve)
- Black pepper, to taste

Method

1. In a large pot, bring water to a boil with salt, onion, bell pepper, garlic, thyme, and tomato paste (if using). Add potatoes (if using) and simmer 8–10 minutes, until just tender.
2. Lower heat to a gentle simmer. Add fish and whole hot peppers.
3. Simmer 6–10 minutes (depending on thickness) until the fish flakes easily. Don't boil hard or the fish will break apart.

4. Turn off heat. Stir in lime juice and black pepper. Taste and adjust salt.
5. Serve hot with lime wedges and a spoon of broth.

Notes: Keep the hot peppers whole for flavor without turning the pot fiery. Simmer gently—hard boiling breaks fish apart. Add lime at the end for the brightest taste.

Recipe — Bahamian Stew Conch (Serve with Johnny Cake)

Dish: Stew Conch (Rich Tomato Gravy)

Ingredients

- 2 lbs. cleaned conch, tenderized and cut into small pieces
- 2 tbsp oil
- 1 medium onion, diced
- 1 green bell pepper, diced
- 2 cloves garlic, minced
- 1 tbsp tomato paste
- 1 (14.5 oz) can diced tomatoes
- 2 cups water (plus more as needed)
- 1 tsp dried thyme
- 1 tsp kosher salt (to taste)
- 1/2 tsp black pepper
- 1 small hot pepper, whole
- Juice of 1 lime

Method

1. Heat oil in a heavy pot over medium heat. Sauté onion and bell pepper until softened, 4–5 minutes. Add garlic and cook 30 seconds.
2. Stir in tomato paste for 1 minute, then add diced tomatoes, water, thyme, salt, pepper, and the whole hot pepper.
3. Add conch. Bring to a gentle simmer, cover, and cook 1 1/2 to 2 hours, stirring occasionally, until conch is tender. Add splashes of water if the pot gets too thick.
4. Turn off heat and stir in lime juice. Remove the whole hot pepper.
5. Serve hot with Johnny Cake for dipping.

Notes: Low and slow is the secret—conch turns tender with time. Keep the hot pepper whole so the stew stays flavorful, not overwhelming. Serve with Johnny Cake to soak up the gravy.

Recipe — Bahamian Johnny Cake (Baked)

Dish: Johnny Cake (Soft Inside, Golden Crust)

Ingredients

- 3 cups all-purpose flour
- 3 tbsp sugar
- 1 tbsp baking powder
- 1 tsp kosher salt
- 4 tbsp butter, melted (plus more for greasing)
- 1 1/4 cups milk (add a splash more if needed)
- 1 large egg

Method

1. Preheat oven to 375°F. Grease a 9-inch round pan (or an 8x8 pan) with butter.
2. In a bowl, whisk flour, sugar, baking powder, and salt.
3. In a second bowl, whisk melted butter, milk, and egg.
4. Pour wet into dry and stir just until combined into a thick batter/dough (don't overmix). If it feels too stiff, add a splash more milk.
5. Spread into the pan and smooth the top. Score into wedges with a knife.
6. Bake 25–35 minutes, until golden and a toothpick comes out clean. Rest 10 minutes, then slice.

Notes: Serve warm for the soft center and best dip. Don't overmix—stir just until combined. Great with stew conch gravy or boiled fish broth.

Recipe — Bahamian Corned Beef & Yellow Grits

Dish: Corned Beef & Yellow Grits (Breakfast-for-Dinner)

Ingredients

- 1 (12 oz) can corned beef
- 1 tbsp oil or butter
- 1 small onion, diced
- 1/2 green bell pepper, diced
- 1 clove garlic, minced (optional)
- 1 small tomato, diced (optional)
- Black pepper, to taste
- **Grits:** 1 cup yellow grits; 4 cups water (or half water/half milk); 1 tsp salt; 2 tbsp butter
- Optional: 1/2 cup grated cheese for grits

Method

1. Grits: Bring water (or water/milk) to a boil with salt. Slowly whisk in grits. Reduce heat to low and simmer 15–20 minutes, stirring often, until thick and smooth. Stir in butter (and cheese if using).
2. Corned beef: Heat oil/butter in a skillet over medium heat. Sauté onion and bell pepper 3–4 minutes. Add garlic 30 seconds.
3. Add corned beef and break it up with a spoon. Cook 4–6 minutes until heated through and slightly browned in spots. Add tomato if using; cook 1 minute more. Season with black pepper.
4. Serve corned beef over a bowl of hot yellow grits.

Notes: Stir grits often on low heat for a smooth texture. Corned beef is already salty—taste before adding salt. This plate is simple, filling, and made for a long day.

Recipe — Cat Island Pan Bread

Dish: Cat Island Pan Bread (Skillet Bread)

Ingredients

- 3 cups all-purpose flour
- 1 tbsp baking powder
- 1 tsp salt
- 2 tbsp sugar
- 3 tbsp butter (melted) or 3 tbsp oil
- 1 1/4 cups water (add a little more if needed)
- Extra butter, for the pan

Method

1. In a bowl, whisk flour, baking powder, salt, and sugar.
2. Stir in melted butter/oil, then add water and mix until you get a soft dough. If it's dry, add water 1 tbsp at a time.
3. Heat a heavy skillet over medium-low and butter it well.
4. Press dough into the skillet (about 1 to 1 1/2 inches thick). Cover with a lid and cook 12–15 minutes, until the bottom is golden.
5. Flip (use a plate if needed), re-butter the pan, and cook the other side 10–12 minutes until cooked through.
6. Rest 10 minutes, then slice. Serve warm.

Notes: Keep the heat medium-low so the center cooks through before the crust gets too dark. If your skillet runs hot, lower the heat and cover to help the middle set. Best served warm for dipping into stew conch gravy or boiled fish broth.

Recipe — Cat Island Flour Cake

Dish: Cat Island Flour Cake (Simple Island Cake)

Ingredients

- 2 cups all-purpose flour
- 2 tsp baking powder
- 1/2 tsp salt
- 1/2 cup (1 stick) butter, softened
- 1 cup granulated sugar
- 2 large eggs
- 3/4 cup evaporated milk (or whole milk)
- 1 tsp vanilla
- Optional: 1 tsp grated lime zest or lemon zest

Method

1. Preheat oven to 350°F. Grease and flour an 8-inch or 9-inch round pan.

2. Whisk flour, baking powder, and salt.

3. Cream butter and sugar until light. Beat in eggs one at a time, then mix in vanilla (and zest if using).

4. Add dry ingredients in 2 additions, alternating with evaporated milk, mixing just until smooth.

5. Bake 30–40 minutes, until golden and a toothpick comes out clean. Cool 10 minutes, then turn out to cool fully.

Notes: This is a simple, tender cake—perfect with Switcha or tea. Don't overmix once the flour goes in. Evaporated milk gives it that classic island richness without needing frosting.

Recipe — Exuma Conch Fritters

Dish: Conch Fritters (Crisp Outside, Tender Inside)

Ingredients

- 1 cup finely chopped conch (cleaned and tenderized)
- 1/2 cup diced onion
- 1/3 cup diced bell pepper
- 1 tbsp minced hot pepper (to taste)
- 2 tbsp chopped parsley
- 1 1/4 cups all-purpose flour
- 2 tsp baking powder
- 1 tsp kosher salt
- 1/2 tsp black pepper
- 1 large egg, beaten
- 3/4 cup water (add a splash more if needed)
- Oil for frying
- Optional: juice of 1/2 lime in batter

Method

1. Heat 2–3 inches of oil in a pot to about 350°F.
2. In a bowl, mix conch, onion, bell pepper, hot pepper, and parsley.
3. In a second bowl, whisk flour, baking powder, salt, and black pepper. Add egg and water and stir to make a thick batter. Fold in the conch mixture (and lime juice if using).
4. Drop batter by tablespoon into hot oil (don't crowd). Fry 3–5 minutes until deep golden.
5. Drain on a rack or paper towels. Serve hot.

Notes: Chop conch small so the fritters stay tender. Keep the oil hot—cool oil makes heavy fritters.

Recipe — Eleuthera Grouper Fingers

Dish: Grouper Fingers (Island-Style Fish Strips)

Ingredients

- 1 1/2 lbs. grouper fillets, cut into strips
- 2 tbsp lime juice
- 1 tsp kosher salt
- 1/2 tsp black pepper
- 1/2 tsp paprika
- 1/2 tsp garlic powder
- 2 large eggs, beaten
- 1 cup all-purpose flour
- 1 cup fine breadcrumbs or crushed crackers
- Oil for frying
- Optional: hot sauce or vinegar-pepper sauce to serve

Method

1. Pat fish dry. Toss with lime juice, salt, pepper, paprika, and garlic powder. Let sit 10 minutes.
2. Set up dredge: flour in one dish, eggs in another, breadcrumbs/crushed crackers in a third.
3. Coat each strip: flour → egg → crumbs. Press crumbs on well.
4. Heat oil to about 350°F. Fry in batches 2–3 minutes per side until golden and cooked through.
5. Drain on a rack or paper towels. Serve hot with lime and sauce.

Notes: Keep strips similar in size so they cook evenly. Fry in batches to keep the coating crisp.

ABOUT THE AUTHOR

A.G. Seymour is a visionary law tutor, compliance specialist, and author of more than twenty-four books. With an LL.M. from the University of Maryland Francis King Carey School of Law, an LL.B. (Hons.), from the University of London, and certification as a Risk & Compliance Management Professional (CRCMP), she brings a rare combination of academic rigor, regulatory insight, and creative storytelling to the study of law.

Her Law in Pieces series reimagines legal education through anatomically structured case dissections, and emotionally resonant pedagogy designed to spark epiphany. Anjanette G. Seymour believes that every student deserves to feel seen, capable, and at home in the law — and she writes with that mission at heart.

Beyond the page, she is a designer, mentor, and advocate for accessible legal learning, weaving art, narrative, and doctrine into a unified legacy of empowerment.